MARKETING TO
MUMS

Katrina McCarter

'Katrina McCarter is one of the leading Australian authorities on marketing to mums. She is the first person to really back her strategies and suggestions with in-depth research. That's what makes *Marketing to Mums* such an impressive and powerful book for anyone serious about success with the huge mum market.'

**Andrew Griffiths, Australia's #1 Small Business
and Entrepreneurial Author**

'Being a mother can be hard enough, and the pressure of the media only makes it more challenging at times. Media is a powerful voice and has the capacity to shape emotions, perceptions and outcomes, and make us feel less than or like we don't belong. On the flipside, it has the power to move and uplift us and it's imperative that brands understand how to achieve this when reaching out to the powerful mum demographic. Brands need more than stereotypes and misnomers if they are to capture our hearts and minds, and ultimately, our wallets. I highly recommend *Marketing to Mums* for anyone striving to do this, and applaud Katrina McCarter for her work in this area. Happy reading.'

**Emma Isaacs, Founder and Global CEO,
Business Chicks (and mother of four)**

'This book should be required reading for any business that sells to mums. Katrina is effectively giving you the blueprint for selling to Australia's most powerful consumers, backed up with loads of practical tips and case studies. It's more than just a book; it's actually a licence to print money!'

**Loren Bartley, Social Media Strategist at Impactiv8 and
Co-Host and Producer of #BusinessAddicts The Podcast**

'*Marketing to Mums* is my new bible. Like seriously carrying it around in my handbag type of book. As a mum in business selling to mums, this book showed me so many things I have got right, and reminded me that there is still loads more that I can do to help connect with my tribe, sell, create raving fans and spread my message of empowering women. If you sell to mums (and who doesn't?) you need this book. In fact, you needed it yesterday.'

Dr Leandra Brady-Walker, Chiropractor, Author, Speaker and The Original Cosmopolitan Hippy

'I love marketing books that match the promise of their title. *Marketing to Mums* excels, teaching you about consumer mums. Valuable insights include learning: who they are, how many, how they shop, their reliance upon social media, and how to engage them commercially. Important trends are revealed. Critically, using case studies and instruction, a practical approach to developing a relevant marketing approach is revealed including topics of brand and product positioning and developing your own online marketing strategy.'

Dr Kevin Argus (PhD), Lecturer in Marketing, Graduate School of Business and Law, RMIT

'Every successful Mumpreneur has within her the unfailing determination, grit and business smarts of a woman like Katrina McCarter. But now, Katrina is helping other success seekers "dodge the landmines" with her personal story of the trials of running her own business. Her light-hearted but honest account offers important business lessons alongside practical advice that's tailored to anyone juggling the challenges of mothering children AND a business. I just wish it was around when I was starting out.'

Bec Derrington, Founder and CEO, SourceBottle.com

'In *Marketing to Mums,* Katrina shares her invaluable insights into the way real Australian mums make purchasing decisions and gives practical advice on how to use this information to increase sales. Over the past five years she has come to know this powerful market sector very well, through her award-winning ecommerce site and more recently through her survey. Katrina's book gives mums a voice and provides a wake-up call to the business community that has been underestimating them for far too long.'

Dr Marcus Tan, CEO and Medical Director, HealthEngine

'Katrina's book is both timely and relevant to marketers and advertisers as we undertake a debate around industry diversity. Findings in a recent report by PwC found the average creative executive is a so called 'Bondi Hipster' and this is a factor in the industry's performance and output. It is therefore not too surprising to see communications and marketing needs to be better at resonating with mums. Katrina's new book, through its practical tips and case studies, will go some way to help this debate as the marketing industry puts strategies in place to address the disconnect between its communications and key sectors such Australia's parents.'

Denise Shrivell, Founder, MediaScope

'*Marketing to Mums* is a brilliant resource for anyone smart enough to target this powerful segment and wanting to do it right. Always looking for ways to create win-win outcomes, Katrina generously leverages her unique assets to provide you with insights and tools that are sure to deliver quick wins in your business.'

Simone Novello, Founder, Partner2GROW.com

'Katrina has become a great friend over the last couple of years as she has also become a part of my advisory team. Katrina is a fantastic operator and is incredibly astute to the world of business and marketing. I greatly value her integrity, honesty, insight and business acumen and her ability to identify opportunities for improvement and growth and foster incredible relationships with all those she comes into contact with.'

Fiona Redding, Founder, The Happiness Hunter
and Co-Host #BusinessAddicts The Podcast

'Prana Chai is an artisan tea blending company catering mostly to cafes and other businesses. The founders employed the services of Katrina McCarter from Marketing to Mums to drive online sales and market directly to the customers drinking our chai. Firstly, Katrina was meticulous in her analysis of the direct sales side of the company. From that research she was able to formulate a detailed plan to achieve our objectives and was extremely diligent in carrying out our plan with professionalism and intelligence at every step. Using Katrina's methodology has made a great improvement to our company and the way we communicate with our customers. She has also been a great source of positive inspiration when facing the challenges of running a business and I absolutely recommend her services.'

Mario Minichilli, Co-Founder, Prana Chai

'Katrina was an absolute lifesaver for my business! When I first contacted her I didn't know where I was going wrong. I had a great product that people loved but I wasn't getting the sales. I was frustrated and had spent a LOT of money on advertising with no results. I was about to give up when Katrina literally came to my rescue. After implementing Katrina's advice I am now fully booked for my events and am having to turn customers away so I am currently looking to expand. She also gave me wonderful advice on how to stay sane while on this business rollercoaster. I cannot recommend Katrina highly enough.'

Sarah Rouche, Founder, Red Cat Science

National Library of Australia Cataloguing-in-Publication entry:

    Creator: McCarter, Katrina, author.
    Title: Marketing to mums: how to sell more to Australia's most powerful consumer / Katrina McCarter.
    ISBN: 9780994634108 (paperback)
    Subjects: Consumers—Research—Australia.
        Mothers—Australia—Economic conditions.
        Consumer behavior—Australia.
        Consumer's preferences—Australia.
        Marketing—Australia.
    Dewey Number: 658.8340994

Book cover design by Julia Kuris of Designerbility
Text design and typesetting by design@bluerinse.com.au
Editorial services by Andrea McNamara
Proofread by Sonja Heijn
Author photo by Jason Malouin of Portrait Store
Printed in Australia by Minuteman Press Prahran 60033

Disclaimer

MARKETING
TO MUMS

The Marketing to Mums survey report compiles information from more than 1800 Australian mums on how they want to be marketed to, as well as their social media habits. It identifies mistakes businesses make when advertising to mums and, in an Australian first, mums tell us what they want marketers to do differently to increase the likelihood of them making a purchase.

Throughout this book, you'll find short grabs from the 2016 survey identified as #inmumswords

The survey findings are significant and a great asset to any business that is serious about attracting mums to their business.

For further information about purchasing this report please go to www.marketingtomums.com.au/2016surveyreport

CONTENTS

If only I knew this when I started ...

The way mums seek and digest information about products and services has changed dramatically in the past decade. The rise in the use of smartphones, the increased reliance on mum-to-mum recommendations and their love of social media have seen many small businesses left behind in their delivery of marketing messages to this powerful segment of the market.

Marketing to Mums: How to sell more to Australia's most powerful consumer is for micro and small business owners that target mums. If you are unsure how to attract new customers to your business, if you feel stuck and don't know how to improve your cash flow, I can show you how to make some simple changes that can really impact your bottom line and don't require lots of time and money. It doesn't matter whether or not you have business qualifications or big marketing budgets; I want to show you how to achieve business success.

I will share my journey from stay-at-home mother of three to successful business owner with over $1,000,000 in transactions in just over two years of operation – all with a marketing investment of $300 per month (and often less). You can do this too by tapping into the most underrated, undervalued consumer segment in the world: mums.

It was by no means an easy journey and I learnt many things along the way, a lot of them the hard way. I often found myself saying, 'If I only knew this when I started ...' so I will share practical examples, tips and learnings so you can power ahead in your business. I am a highly practical person and I want to share things you can apply to your business and know you can get results.

This book is a step-by-step guide to driving sales without spending a fortune. It is particularly suited to business owners who have been operating for more than a year and currently invest under $5000 in advertising per annum.

I will guide you through an eight-step framework that will get you analysing your business and getting to know your customers better, all with a view to presenting your product or service in a way that will appeal to mums. You'll be able to identify subtle changes you can make in the way you interact with mums, and I'll show you practical ways to build your community and generate more sales. You will see the power of partnerships and how they can be applied to so many different aspects of your business to deliver growth with very little financial investment.

There are actionable activities at the end of each stage with a focus on quick wins.

I know your life as a small business owner can often be overwhelming because I've experienced this feeling myself, so *Marketing to Mums: How to sell more to Australia's most powerful consumer* is designed so that you can do small things to make a big difference while you learn more about this powerful consumer group. Once you have worked through the framework, I have no doubt that you will have a deeper appreciation of mums and the incredible contribution they make to your business and our economy.

After applying these tools you will enjoy a better night's sleep knowing that you have a solid affordable strategy in place to generate more customers and deliver more sales. I encourage you to take this opportunity to reflect on your business, identify where you want it to be and develop a plan for how to get there.

Getting to know mums as a consumer group will be a rewarding experience on every level. I've thoroughly enjoyed the journey.

part 1

THE POWER
OF MUM

Mums are the powerhouse behind the Australian economy. According to Canadean, mums control $132 billion in consumer spending in Australia every year. Staggering statistic, isn't it? If mums were an industry they would be the largest contributor to GDP in this country.

The mum market is already large and it's growing. There are over 6,227,200 mums in Australia with a further 140,000 women becoming mothers every year. These women are the primary decision makers when it comes to almost everything. Think about this. Not only is mum responsible for the vast majority of groceries being purchased, she is also deciding which house the family should live in, where to go on holiday, what car the family needs, which healthcare provider to select, which electrician and plumber to use, what computer and phone to buy. The list goes on. Mums have enormous control over spending.

Mums' purchasing is not limited to the household either. Women are entering the small business world at twice the rate of men with more than 314,000 mums controlling businesses in Australia. In that context, mums are also controlling the spending decisions on advertising, office supplies, cars, insurance, computers, phones and legal services.

Mums have enormous influence over the spending in other consumer segments too. They share brand and product shortcomings and recommendations with other mums, family members and friends.

You cannot afford to underestimate, undervalue, misunderstand or ignore these powerful consumers, decision makers and influencers. Yet surprisingly many marketers and business owners often do just that. How many advertising messages for computers, electronics and cars are targeted at men?

Imagine if these organisations directed the majority of their campaigns at mums. Why invest so many funds in targeting the wrong market segment?

I passionately believe businesses need to recognise the value of mum and then use her influence to grow their business. I believe that dedicating time to understanding mums, nurturing relationships and then tailoring your communications to meet mums' needs will deliver enormous financial rewards for Australian businesses.

Don't you want a part of the action?

MY STORY

Now you know that mums are powerful consumers and that the scope of their purchasing decisions is broad, I'll share a little bit about how I came to know this market so well and how this led to the development of my eight-step framework. You'll see why I'm passionate about representing mums and my aim is for you to glean a few things you can apply in your own business to increase your sales right now.

It wasn't all smooth sailing for my first business, Bubbler, a group buying site with family deals. There were plenty of lessons that I learnt the hard way, and I'm happy to share them with you so you can avoid them. But I'm actually very grateful for some of the mistakes I made; because of them I am now more resilient, a more creative problem solver and ultimately, a better business owner.

Embrace your mistakes. Nothing is more powerful than accepting and admitting the error, then working hard to fix it or provide an alternative positive outcome.

Passion for business

The seeds for business ownership were sown early in my life. My brother, my mother, my father, my uncle, my aunty are all microbusiness owners. It seemed a natural course for me to take. I was an enterprising kid – the one holding garage sales, making jewellery to sell at the markets, always with at least one part-time job.

My parents separated when I was young and my mother was determined that I have a solid understanding of money – how to earn it, how to manage it and how to make more of it. From the age of 12 I was submitting quarterly reports to my mum detailing how much money I'd need for schoolbooks, excursions, pocket money and so on and she'd issue it and I'd be entirely responsible for managing it. At my engagement party, Mum had great delight in sharing those financial reports with my fiancé, highlighting my financial independence. We laugh about it now but those reports allowed me to understand planning and managing a cash flow. More so, I learnt opportunity summary: that by choosing to go out to X I'd not have enough money to do Y.

At 14 I fell in love with New York, fuelled by media reports and hearing exotic stories from my aunty who lived there. To me, New York really represented a place where you could create anything. My mum was always very focused on following your passion and dreaming big so I got myself a job at Kentucky Fried Chicken working for $3.28 an hour to make my dream come true. By 16 I had saved my airfare and a bit of spending money and off I went with Mum. I was exceptionally lucky that I had a mother who allowed me to realise a big dream early on in life. It has been a critical factor in developing my business mindset. Big dreams can be realised.

I didn't go straight into setting up my own business. After completing a Bachelor of Business majoring in Marketing, I had a corporate life for many years in Melbourne, working for large organisations representing some of Australia's biggest brands including Tim Tam, Pedigree, Pal and Whiskas. All of the products I worked with targeted the key grocery decision maker: mums. I loved the science behind each brand and negotiating its shelf space and promotions so more mums could purchase our products. One particular organisation I worked for, Mars Petcare, was an excellent training ground for going into business. They believed strongly in giving their employees great freedom so our small team could act very independently, almost like running your own business.

Later, after a Masters of Business Administration specialising in International Business, I felt equipped to step out and do something on my own. To me, success

> My childhood taught me two things: creative problem solving and dreaming big.

is defined as being able to create and run a business from scratch. It has always been very high on my bucket list. I am energised hearing about other people's businesses and seeing their journey from idea to fruition. Often, it doesn't feel like work because I'm just following my passion.

The parenting transformation

In 2003 I became a mum and boy, was it life changing! I had hugely underestimated the transition required in moving from my corporate career to life at home with a baby. We added another two children to our tribe in reasonably quick succession and I made the decision to be the primary caregiver for the first five years of their lives.

I spent my days in the park with other parents, predominantly mums, and unconsciously I started to understand the depths of their issues. Some of these things were my issues too, of course. I was able to see the key problems facing mums and how those varied from mum to mum. It was very clear to me that all mums were not the same and yet we were often lumped into a generic group. It was around this time that I began to experience how out of touch marketers were in marketing their products to me, a mum. I felt strongly that they didn't understand my issues and their depictions of a mum were really off base. In short, it became very evident that mums were being blasted by poor advertising that was just 'noise'.

The businesswoman in me could see that businesses were (and still are) missing out on achieving greater sales conversions as a result of their inability to connect with mums: the most powerful consumer group.

Getting a good deal

Fast forward to 2011. I was living in Perth raising my three kids with my husband. It was meant to be a twelve-month break from Melbourne to enjoy warmer weather and I relished the opportunity to spend time with my family. My social life revolved around a game of cards with a few of my girlfriends. One particular evening they were all talking about some deal they had bought online and how they were saving so much money and enjoying all these fun things to do.

Never one to want to miss out, I immediately signed up and started buying from the group buying sites the girls had been talking about. Essentially, I could purchase a voucher from a business at half-price or more and redeem it directly with the merchant. Businesses were using the group buying platform to increase their product awareness and to bring new customers into their business immediately. I could see this acted as a quick fix for cash flow issues, smoothing out seasonal factors, and was great for launching a new business or product. However, before long my inbox was being filled with lame and irrelevant deals for endless IPL treatments and photobooks. My enterprising brain immediately saw an opportunity: no one was catering for mums. No one was offering family deals.

Who says I can't?

Have you ever been told you can't do something? For some people, being told they are not capable of achieving something stops them from trying, but it merely spurs me on. I love the challenge of doing what other people don't believe is possible.

When I announced that I was going to start up a group buying site for families, I got a lukewarm reception. Few people knew about my corporate background in sales and marketing and I think they looked at this announcement as a little brazen. On top of that, now that the group buying sites had been around for six months, people were freely sharing all their bad experiences with poor deals, product quality, customer service and the like. I was not deterred. I saw a clear opportunity to deliver value to families through relevant family deals.

Because I was spending a bit of time with other mothers, I was also aware of the need to fundraise for schools and playgroups, a burden that usually fell on mums. If I could build in a donation program to my group buying idea, then I would be helping mums support their local community, enabling families to donate 5 per cent of their purchase price to an approved recipient. In other words, I could see the opportunity for my business to act as a silent fundraiser and that would be another reason for mums to visit my site. No one else was doing that.

Finding the cash

So I had this great idea and the motivation but I didn't have all the money. In Perth, everyone knew me as a stay-at-home mum of three. Initially I paced the streets of St Georges Terrace having coffee with potential investors and I was reasonably well received. People were polite but I could tell it wasn't for them. I remember my first meeting where I took a successful entrepreneur out for coffee in a cafe in West Perth. I was very uncomfortable, realising I was out of my depth and I asked all the wrong questions. I ended up red-faced and overwhelmed about how I was going to make my vision a reality. He was lovely, very polite and encouraging but I could tell that this approach wasn't going to get the results I wanted. While those who came out for a coffee with me were excited about online shopping, it was also unknown and unfamiliar territory for them. People felt more comfortable riding the mining and resource boom in Western Australia.

Obviously I was going to need another strategy. I really didn't know what that would be but I knew if I just kept going I'd find a way. While I contemplated my next move, I progressed the business as far as I could. I had identified that I needed someone with great technical know-how if I was going to successfully enter this market. There was a dad at school who had headed up a local IT firm and I engaged him to help me prepare my functional IT requirements.

Colin and I worked very well together. We shared similar values about wanting to contribute to our local community and he loved the giving-back nature of the donation program. He became my first investor. Not only that, he was able to introduce me to his business partner from another venture who also came on board. This gave me the confidence to approach another two small business owners who also got on board. We had lift-off!

Bubbler was born.

Positioning the business

When I told friends that I was launching this business, I was overwhelmed by their comments about negative experiences using a group buying site. Poor service, inability to get a refund, dodgy businesses. I heard them all.

It became very apparent to me that if I was going to be successful I needed to focus on superior customer service. The customers needed to know that I was a trustworthy business.

I was going to be a late entrant in this market, so I had a good look at the existing 40 or so group buying sites. I already knew there was no site dedicated to families – they

MISTAKE #1

ADVERTISING IN PRINT

Growing Bubbler's database was our number one priority when we launched the business. I placed an advertisement in a parenting print magazine with the aim of attracting at least 300 new subscribers. I may as well have thrown $300 out of the window. It did absolutely nothing. When I queried it with the publication, I was informed that I really needed to commit to three months of advertising, costing $900, to test if it would work. I didn't have the time or money. I quickly learnt that mums today are more likely to be on their phones surfing the internet than reading a magazine. I was an online business so my marketing mediums needed to be online too. I needed to ensure that all my marketing efforts were only a simple click away to my website.

were all mainstream sites targeting anyone and everybody. I felt if we entered that space we would just be more noise in the group buying industry and that it was important to differentiate ourselves from the outset. So rather than being a family deal site within the group buying industry, we looked to position our business as the only family deal site within the *parenting* industry. We networked within this industry.

From the word go, I knew that we needed to have some credibility and that people needed to trust us. Capturing a mum's trust is not easy so I looked for a partner. We sought a partnership with the local playgroup association. They were a reputable organisation so there was an assumption that we must be okay to buy from.

Finding partners

For me, business is all about collaboration and partnerships. This idea was probably fostered early in my career at Mars Petcare where I was a national business manager looking after a major supermarket chain account. Our sales director would release some promotional monies to invest in the account he felt could get the best rate of return on his investment. By understanding how my buyer was measured within his business, we were able to work together and take a team approach and secure those funds. By working together, we were able to secure significant investment into large scale promotions within this retail supermarket chain, generating considerable additional sales. Both my buyer and I exceeded our respective performance measures.

I took this team-based approach into my own business. I had investment but we were launching without the luxury of big marketing budgets. We needed to be resourceful so I set out to see who I could work alongside. Firstly, I looked for businesses that shared the same target market as mine but were not in competition with me, then I crafted a simple three-page proposal including how it would work and what each party would do. The conversion rate from these approaches was incredibly high because I was able to accurately assess what was important to the other party, and then balance the outcomes so they would be equal for each player.

Initially I looked to partner with playgroup associations because I wanted to position my business as being credible and trustworthy. As my key donation beneficiaries, these state playgroup associations were able to raise monies (great for them) and I was able to position my business (great for me). For a new player in the industry, this was significant.

As my business grew, my partnering needs changed; I needed to build my email database list. Again, I looked for businesses that operated within the parenting space and that were not competing with me. I looked at running a joint competition. The only costs to me would be my time in locating a suitable prize sponsor and negotiating the partnership, and paying a graphic designer to prepare the competition graphics.

My first six months after launching Bubbler were not without some unexpected hiccups. I was adjusting to the rigours of needing to have three deal campaigns secured each week. Come Monday, Wednesday and Friday, mums were waiting to see what new thing they could discover and enjoy on Bubbler. I was a one-man band and was still juggling the needs of my three kids, working school hours and then in the evening as soon as they went to sleep.

Making valuable connections

Gone are the days when you could grow your business alone. Collaboration is the key to growth and it's very important that you reach out and connect with other people in your industry. Collaborating is not only the fastest way to grow your business, it can also be loads of fun, particularly if you enjoy meeting people.

I was able to secure my first few partnerships because I had great connections with people who respected and trusted me. It really highlighted to me the importance of networking. Just because I was in Perth didn't mean I couldn't develop relationships with key players in the eastern states – Facebook and the phone took care of that.

In fact, I have made my most valuable connections by being very brave and cold calling people I admire and asking them how they did it. If I read an interesting article about an entrepreneur in the paper or online which interests me, I reach out.

Charlie Caruso is Australia's gen Y disruptor. A few years ago I read an article in the weekend paper about how she had started a radio station for families. Liking what she was doing and seeing we were targeting the same market, I emailed her. We hit it off, shared similar beliefs and quickly found that we shared complementary skill sets. We subsequently caught up every few months for brainstorming sessions to thrash out business ideas and create strategies. I now consider Charlie a friend and we've spent many hours brainstorming business projects and one day we just might work together. And it all started by being brave and sending a cold email.

Another time I had observed the work of an entrepreneur working interstate. I thought her idea was unique and I like her creative approach to business. We connected through Facebook on a Friday night and messaged back and forth about our ideal customers and how our business models worked. The following week we commenced discussions about a marketing partnership with another shared connection. This activity did take some time and negotiation to pull off, however it was worth every minute. It was a huge success for all parties and we added 7000 new subscribers to our business over three weeks with under $100 spent on graphics. This was an amazing return on investment and wouldn't have happened if I hadn't spent time developing relationships with key people within my industry.

Over the past four years I have connected with many thought leaders and influencers in various sectors via LinkedIn, people I am now able to call upon for advice in specific areas. I am also involved in lots of online business groups which keeps me ahead of trends and changes within my industry. Working alone can be isolating but I found that meeting like-minded business people gave me a network and community, and enabled me to stay on top of the political landscape and understand business alliances. I've had wonderful collaborations with mutual gains, and over time, many of those initial partnerships with business owners have become friendships.

MISTAKE # 2

NOT DOING A THOROUGH CHECK ON A PARTNER

In the first six months, I entered into a deal campaign for an indoor play centre that was relocating. When we signed a legally binding agreement, the fitout was not yet completed. I was holidaying in Coral Bay when the deal went live. It sold well, as mums are always keen to try something new, but then within the first 24 hours I received seven complaints about the venue, claiming it was unsafe for children. My heart sank. I put myself in the shoes of my community and thought about how they would want this addressed. I knew that if someone had a bad experience on our website, they wouldn't come back. I returned to Perth, inspected the venue and agreed with my community. I then wrote a letter to every single person who purchased a voucher.

cont.

2

'Given the inability of X to deliver upon the advertised deal and the concerns raised by our customers, Bubbler Deals has made the decision to refund ALL purchases for this deal. No action is required by you and all transactions will be refunded within three working days. Your voucher will no longer be valid. We thank you for providing us with feedback on this deal and hope we have acted in your best interests. We greatly apologise for any inconvenience caused to you and will work hard to learn from this experience and serve you better in the future.'

We were immediately inundated with emails from our members congratulating us on our action. We turned a really negative harmful event into a great PR story. By putting myself in my customers' shoes, I was able to see their safety concerns, admit my mistake and take prompt action. My community now had faith that if something went wrong with their voucher purchases, I had their back and would step in and support them. It really strengthened our trust and credibility.

I always look to learn from experience. I find it eases the pain and ensures I don't repeat the mistake. More so, this experience highlighted the importance of choosing a good partner and introducing some controls to tighten our vetting process. It allowed us to show our commitment to our customers and position our business as being customer service focused. This mistake enabled me to learn some powerful customer service strategies which I live by today.

The first stumbling block

My husband, a scientist, was looking for a new challenge and with his family based in Melbourne and my love of big cities, it seemed natural for us to return to the East Coast of Australia. So midway through 2013, I relocated the business. We had enjoyed great success in Western Australia and I was keen to see if we could become a really national player, and thought being closer to some of the big brands could help us take things up a notch.

I took active steps to prepare the business for growth. After working from home for so long I wanted to introduce a bit more structure into my day so I spent the first few months of 2014 setting up an office in Collingwood which was nice and close to home, hiring our first employee and really looking at our systems.

I also started training some contractors. My most important contractor was for social media. After years of spending eight hours on a Sunday finding content and scheduling posts, I realised I needed some assistance. If I was going to prepare the business for growth I needed to free up some of my time for more strategic activities. Relinquishing my social media duties was by no means easy but I had been watching a particular person closely for the previous twelve months. She understood the power and responsibility of managing a community and its impact on our sales. We commenced a three-month trial so I could see how it would work and measured sales so I could see drops and community losses. We set up a Facebook group where we could communicate any messages. We also set up a weekly schedule of posts after reviewing page insights and discussing optimum timings. I maintained control over anything client related but the sourcing and scheduling of engaging content and promoting deal campaigns became her domain. It turned out to be a winning formula.

Through this process I have improved my own understanding of social media, identifying winning content and the issues that really drive my community to action. It became a wonderful opportunity for them to learn more about me, the person behind the business, and equally for me to learn more about them – what's important to them, what frustrates them, what they like or dislike. These insights empowered me to provide more tailored information for our clients and ensured we maximised the return for them too.

My plan was to launch local Melbourne deals in categories which had proved successful in Perth. By June we were offering one or two local deals each week. But sourcing these deals was much harder in Melbourne, partly because many businesses had already firmly established links with our competition. Also, Melbourne has a much broader geographical spread than Perth, so the voucher sales were lower than we would have liked.

Our Melbourne database was spread out and unwilling to travel, unlike our Perth subscribers.

We had hit our first stumbling block. The return on the time invested just wasn't worth it. This was all rather disappointing and challenging.

Pivoting the business

In June 2014 I was feeling really conflicted with my business. I had been sitting on an idea for a new income stream for some months and I had not been able to gain clarity on it. I was conscious that many group buying sites were folding up after succumbing to 'deal fatigue' and 'inbox overload' and I wanted to safeguard our business against that and see it continue to prosper. I knew I needed to innovate but I was unsure how to achieve this without potentially damaging my business.

'Pivoting' is a familiar word to entrepreneurs. If your business model isn't working, you pivot to plan B, applying your insights to a new direction.

I spent a lot of time listening to what prospective partners had to say about their marketing objectives. By listening to them, I made a surprising discovery: they found Western Australia a really hard market to break in to. Over and over again the same story was being repeated. Big brands wanted to connect with Perth mums because they knew they spent big but they were finding it increasingly difficult to break in. These brands were constantly being seen as 'corporate' or 'national' and Perth mums like to support local. And so Bubbler's Perth roots became our secret weapon amongst mainstream competitors. Now, not only did we have our 5 per cent donation program, we also were armed with our strong, engaged community of Perth mums.

Through this process I had identified that there was a large segment of businesses we weren't attracting with our group buying model. Big brands didn't want to be associated with a deal site or discounter so I had an idea to launch an advertising platform on our site where businesses could connect with our community of 150,000 mums without the need to discount their product by 40 per cent or more. This idea would see my business model change from a group buying site to a hybrid shopping website where I would also offer brands connection to our mums via newsletter and social media advertising. I was very mindful that there was considerable risk in progressing this idea. It had the potential to confuse our customer base and I knew that a confused customer never buys. This new approach had the potential to ostracise our community.

I sought advice, and I was very lucky with the timing of a mentoring opportunity. In 2014 I won a national social media award and part of my prize was a 30-minute mentoring session with Fiona Redding, a life and business strategist. Her business is The Happiness Hunter, where people, predominantly business enthusiasts, get out and take a walk in nature, and talk about their roadblocks and opportunities. Our 30-minute session quickly spilled over to 90 minutes in a very robust discussion about this proposed business pivot. We had a long chat about the pros and cons and she convinced me that in order to achieve great success you need to risk something. I took comfort knowing that I was small enough that we were nimble and if it didn't work I could always recover and continue as Australia's only dedicated group buying site for families.

On the back of that phone call, in June 2014 we launched a group newsletter where we promoted ten sales by other businesses and directed traffic to their websites. I attracted a whole new group of larger clients including the likes of Cotton On Kids, Booktopia and Bonds. The advertising platform didn't encroach on our deal campaigns, our community loved getting a whole lot of sales in one newsletter and it delivered higher open rates and worked to increase engagement. The results were amazing. Within months, the advertising platform was contributing 30–50 per cent of Bubbler's monthly revenue and I had doubled my income!

Not only were we happy but so were our new clients. One national retailer ran a campaign in our group newsletter for a ladies vintage bike. The feature resulted in a 33:1 return on their investment and further advertising bookings with that client.

As an aside, I now walk with Fiona Redding's group each week. This is yet another example of how important it has been on my business journey to build relationships along the way.

MISTAKE # 3

NOT LISTENING TO MY GUT

My gut instincts have served me well to date. I've learnt to trust that if something doesn't feel right, more often than not it isn't. Not so long ago I was involved in a marketing partnership that had very surprising outcomes. The competition yielded 2900 entries yet the prize was relatively small and the other businesses involved were not large. Immediately alarm bells rang; I took action, discovering hundreds of robotic spam entries. Needless to say I severed the partnership immediately. In the early days of Bubbler, I would have been so thrilled at a surprising response, I might have turned the sound down on those alarm bells.

Pushing myself

By late 2014 I felt ready to do Bubbler alone, without my team of investors. I was always keen to push myself. To me, entrepreneurship is the ultimate career test, one that will reveal what you are made of. It is certainly a rollercoaster ride and your ability to lean in and hang in there will see you reap great rewards.

My business journey so far was pretty good. I had started the business, moved my family interstate, pivoted the business model and was enjoying good growth. I felt as though I had grown some wings and was ready to test myself and go it alone. This was a big move for me. I recognised that I wouldn't have been able to launch the business without my business partners so letting them go spoke volumes about what I had achieved.

I made an offer to my shareholders in October 2014. The timing was right. We had always spoken about a three-year exit but I felt unfinished with the business. After the pivot I felt that there was so much more scope to grow the business.

Throughout January 2015 we had meetings and discussions around the offer and by the end of the month the offer had been accepted by three shareholders. Paperwork was completed by March. I felt as though I had grown up. What I appreciated more than anything were the words of one of my investors who said he would like me to approach him again with any future ventures as he would be interested in investing again. That vote of confidence really propelled me further to push through boundaries.

I was definitely ready for new adventures.

Taking a risk for success

After trading for three and a half years I noticed that businesses came to Bubbler with the same three issues. Firstly, they needed customers and they needed them fast. Secondly, they lacked the expertise to find them. Thirdly, they were so busy working operationally within their business that they didn't have time to do anything about it. They often presented in a state of anxiety, concerned about their cash flow and I felt many were questioning the long-term viability of their businesses.

I realised that I now had the expertise to deliver the customers they wanted, but I started thinking it would be even better if I could prevent business owners from experiencing such anxiety in the first place. Wouldn't it be great if I could teach them how to market to mums? This idea niggled away at me over the next six months. I consulted with mentors and did lots of thinking about what I wanted, identifying what I valued and what was important to me. I knew the idea of coaching and consulting to others about how to target mums was an excellent one. There were a few agencies around who focused on women but there was very little that focused solely on mums. It surprised me. Surely if mums were such a powerful consumer segment, someone would already be offering services to assist businesses in this market?

I identified that the two things that interested me most in my working life were women (specifically mums) and business. I felt passionately that there was a new way to communicate to mums, and that many businesses were missing out on significant sales by not being educated about this. I felt that I could make a big difference by showing them how they could build better relationships with mums to improve their bottom line, and that it needn't cost a fortune. And with that, I took a leap of faith in late 2015 and launched my marketing and research consultancy, Marketing to Mums.

With the launch of the consulting practice I had a spring in my step again, a spring I didn't realise I had lost in working within Bubbler. This was a significant personal learning: I loved the creation of a business and realising a vision, but once that vision was realised I was ready to move on to new challenges. But this also created an internal conflict for me: do I abandon my community that I worked so hard to grow and pursue new desires? It caused me endless sleepless nights. I felt very torn. In the end, I recognised the value in how much I had learned through the Bubbler experience, and that it was time for me to risk something again, in pursuit of new success. The way I saw it was that by directing 100 per cent of my time to the consultancy, I would be doing preventative work with businesses, rather than what was so often 'last resort' work. That was very appealing.

I have a thirst for learning and Marketing to Mums allows me to have that constant learning. I work with clients for twelve months and take on a specific project. I learn their industry's nuances and apply my insights and learnings to their business which results in significant sales increases and then I move on, ready for the next project. I back this up with frequent research into mums, the way they communicate and how they want to be marketed to. My consultancy business undertook the first major survey of Australian mums in April and May 2016 and it is clear that mums want businesses to hear them and change the way they do things. Armed with the voices of these Australian mums, I love showing businesses a new way to market to the powerhouse of our economy.

As entrepreneurs we need to get comfortable with risk. To grow as a person and expand your business you must take risks.

10 MUM TRENDS

Mums have changed in the past ten years. They're a diverse, sophisticated and experienced consumer group that presents many challenges for businesses, but on the flipside, many opportunities exist for those prepared to engage in understanding these changes. I want to spend a bit of time looking at ten significant trends we have seen in mums over the past few years so you can identify how they might be impacting your business.

Throughout this section, I will be sharing many results from the Marketing to Mums 2016 survey. We surveyed more than 1800 Australian mums online about the way they want to be marketed to and their use of social media. If you want to attract more mums to your product or service, you will find the insights particularly useful.

Trend 1 – Technology

Mums have embraced new technology with gusto. Mum loves her smartphone, and increased internet access means she can control her busy life from her handbag. Mum loves the feeling of being connected to her world. Bills can be paid, appointments noted; she can organise kids' sport commitments, access her Facebook and Instagram accounts, make arrangements with friends, entertain the kids, take photos, research products and brands, enter competitions, review catalogues and shop online. It provides her with enormous convenience and flexibility.

In 2014 Reborn Research reported that 65 per cent of the population has a smartphone but 80 per cent of women aged 25–54 years have a smartphone. In two short years, smartphone usage amongst mums has grown significantly with the Marketing to Mums survey reporting more than 90 per cent of mums own a smartphone, with iPhone being their smartphone of choice.

Mum uses her smartphone to browse and window shop much like she might have done a decade ago in shopping centres and shopping strips around the country. This is supported by Criteo research published in 2016 which reports that 37 per cent of desktop buyers browsing the retailer's site use other devices prior to purchase. Bigger screens have made a difference here, as has easy free WiFi access.

Mum also finds her smartphone is an invaluable tool for reviewing pricing and checking availability on products that interest her. She wants minimal clicks to purchase and easy payment options. Mum loves PayPal as she only needs to remember her sign-in rather than having to get out her wallet and enter in all the credit card information.

Mums are now exceptionally well informed about the problems, features and pricing of your brand and that of your competitors before they even speak to you.

MEET KATIE

Katie is a mum of three kids. She owns two businesses and is also the primary carer for her children, meaning she's the one who ensures they get off to school on time, is home when they get back from school, and she taxis them off to their various after-school activities. Katie's smartphone is by her side 24/7 except for two hours on a Thursday when she enjoys her mid-week technology detox. She does this so she can reconnect with the world and not feel compelled to answer calls, respond to clients and generally be at someone else's beck and call. Katie uses her phone to check banking, take photos of her kids (and a few selfies!), research things (normally prices on products she wants) and check her social media accounts.

Katie loves her smartphone although her kids tell her she is on it too often. She finds it so easy to check emails and moderate her social media page on the go. She once lost her smartphone and felt completely disconnected from the world, and had sheer panic about people not being able to reach her. She had a new one within 24 hours.

Trend 2 – Social media

Mum has a love affair with social media; it's her little bit of daily 'me time'. She uses social media to keep in touch with friends, discover new products or services, feel connected to the world, read the news and get advice from other mums.

The Marketing to Mums survey found that 91 per cent of mums access their social media accounts daily, with the following frequency:

→ 61 per cent access their social media up to ten times each day

→ 19 per cent check in 11–20 times each day

→ 11 per cent claim to check their social media 21 times or more each day

It seems that FOMO (Fear of Missing Out) is alive and well with mums wanting to keep abreast of trends and new products, services and events. Their favourite time to access social media is after the kids go to bed when they can enjoy some uninterrupted viewing. Equally mums say they will jump onto social media any chance they get. A whopping 86 per cent of respondents feel that social media is addictive.

Despite very solid use of Instagram, YouTube and Pinterest, over a seven-day period mums identify Facebook as their favourite social media platform (70 per cent) followed by Instagram (15 per cent).

Mums use social media to hold brands accountable too. A few years ago a mum complained to Target on their Facebook page about the 'tramp like' clothing for young girls available in their stores. She received 54,000 likes and 3000 comments supporting her claims. Social media is an empowering tool which now sees mums' views matter.

Last year on the Bubbler Facebook page, I posted about an unpleasant experience I had with my daughter. Dining at a well-known cafe chain I was asked to prove (with a birth certificate or passport) my 11-year-old daughter's age so she could order from the children's menu which was advertised for 12 years and under. I was instructed it was 'company policy' that parents need to prove their child's age! I was irate. My daughter is tall for her age and entered puberty earlier than some; I was very annoyed that this guy behind the counter was drawing attention to an already self-conscious 11-year-old. We left immediately and have not returned. Mums went into overdrive expressing their outrage at my experience, calling for me to name and shame the organisation. They wanted to take collective action against the cafe chain. Understanding the damage this could cause, instead I reported it to their head office who were very apologetic

> Due to using social networks, online consumers are not just buyers anymore; they are critics, experts, advocates, and influencers.
>
> *Alex Gonzalez, CEO and co-founder of Chatalog*

MEET ROS

Ros is a single mother of two boys aged six and 11 years. She works fulltime as a public health professional in the not-for-profit sector in Melbourne. Ros is passionate about health and prevention, and also runs a swim and resort sun protection label for women called Aquacove®. Ros accesses social media multiple times a day, typically in the morning and then evenings. She uses Facebook and Instagram to keep up with friends as well as to promote her business. She mostly connects with like-minded mums and networks with other women running their own businesses especially to put a call out for help or to find a contact. She likes that social media can be responsive as it allows her to get things done faster. Plus she relies on the birthday reminders to ensure she doesn't miss making a call or acknowledging a friend's special day. Ros belongs to numerous online groups for mums and particularly follows bloggers via Facebook. The groups she participates in depend very much on her life stage and the business development opportunities.

and confirmed it was definitely not company policy. I chose not to use the influence I held over my community of 150,000 mums to cause damage for this cafe chain. I was satisfied that the head office was going to retrain the person in question. I share my experience to highlight how one bad experience can potentially be shared and have devastating impacts for a business. It is imperative that your staff, the face of your business, understand the essence of your brand, what it values and how to handle delicate customer interactions.

Social media is providing mums with a voice in the media too. It is empowering mums to tell businesses what they don't want brands to do in the future, providing great insights and learnings for businesses willing to listen to them. On Mother's Day 2016, a blog article titled 'Fuck You, Mother's Day' went viral, ranting about what mums really want for Mother's Day. Mums around the world used social media to share the article and tell the world that they don't want sleepwear, candles or cookbooks.

Trend 3 – Mum-to-mum recommendations

Mum seeks authenticity and can sniff out a hidden sales message in an instant. She is turned off by celebrity endorsements, preferring to hear another mum talk about why they like a business.

Not only are mums changing the way they receive their marketing communications, we have also seen a real move away from corporate sales messages in favour of seeking mum-to-mum recommendations. A mum-to-mum recommendation ranks as the second highest influence when making a purchasing decision, according to the Marketing to Mums survey.

Mums are actively seeking recommendations from 'real' mums everywhere they go. Head to the park and mums are talking about brands. It's the same at playgroup, at school drop-off, in coffee shops around the country – anywhere they meet up with other mums, they are sharing advice and recommendations, and stories about a bad customer service experience with a business.

Mums get even more active online. In the Marketing to Mums survey, 66 per cent of mums claimed to be in social media groups which are just for mums. It is here that mums are talking about brands and products they like or dislike, asking for advice and solutions to their problems. The groups they belong to typically reflect the stage their children are at.

MEET HARRIET

Harriet is a busy mum of five children aged between ten and 17 living in Brisbane. She 'knows everyone' in her local community and is passionate about her family. She has a great eye for fashion and is seen as a woman of great style. Harriet is a powerful consumer. She has spent many years shopping in stores and online and understands quality and value when she sees it. In fact it is very rare for a day to go by without a trip to the shops for food, fashion or both. She loves to meet people and likes to share her views. She is an influencer amongst her wide network, and is seen as a go-to person for advice on all sorts of things from what to wear and where to buy it, to which builder to use for your next renovation and what car to buy. She's only too happy to tell people what brands and businesses she likes and she's even more vocal about those she doesn't. Now that her children are getting older and becoming more independent Harriet uses her skills to assist other mums to find the right skincare. She likes that her employer's values are in line with her values. In two short years she has progressed quickly through the ranks and now manages her own team. She couldn't imagine working anywhere else.

Trend 4 – Social proof

Mum wants to evaluate whether a business is worthy of her dollars before making a purchase. As well as seeking mum-to-mum recommendations, she looks for ratings, reviews and testimonials.

Mums have become great researchers over the past decade and they actively search for 'social proof' before buying: authentic third party endorsement of a business or product. In the Marketing to Mums survey, mums claimed the number one influence on whether they purchase a product or service is the quality and authenticity of ratings, reviews and testimonials. Prior to making a purchase, mums are likely to search for reviews about the business online, checking the company website for testimonials and looking at their Facebook page to see what star rating they have been given. Mums want to minimise any risk associated with their purchase and achieve the perfect solution to whatever problem they are solving.

75% of Australian mums claim to have made a purchase online in the past 14 days.

Marketing to Mums survey 2016

MEET AMIE

Amie is a 36-year-old stay-at-home mum of three kids aged under ten and lives in Melbourne. She studies nursing part-time and hopes to start working as soon as her youngest is off at school. Amie is an avid shopper with a keen eye for style and likes to achieve 'the look' without the expense. She is a devoted Kmart and eBay fan and she's active in social media groups where other mums share their views on brands. Amie recently went to purchase a new bike for her eldest son. She first went to eBay to check out what was available. Once decided on a brand she liked, she then went online to look for reviews of the business she was considering purchasing from. After reading all 28 reviews and testimonials on their Facebook page, she went ahead with the purchase. Amie reads reviews that appear genuine because she believes it reduces the risk that she might be buying the wrong product. She can pick a fake review in a flash and then avoids dealing with the business altogether.

MEET DONNA

Donna is a mum of three young children under seven and she works fulltime in an HR role in a Melbourne security firm. Each week, Donna has her fruit and vegetables delivered from Aussie Farmers Direct and her groceries delivered from Woolworths. She also purchases all the kids' birthday gifts online and has even purchased a fireplace online. Rarely does she get out to shop – it's just too hard to cart her three little kids into the stores. She loves shopping online as it is easy and can be done at times which are convenient for her. Predominantly she uses her phone to search for products on the go but when she's at home in front of the television after the kids have gone to bed she searches on her iPad in the commercial breaks.

Trend 5 – Online shopping

Mum loves shopping online. She can make a purchase at her convenience, unencumbered by kids.

The arrival of online shopping in Australia has completely changed the way consumers make transactions. IBISWorld, the largest provider of industry data, reports that in 2016, online retailing accounts for more than $16 billion with double digit growth year on year. Mums have embraced the convenience of shopping online. They love how easy it is to search a product by price and that they can purchase from almost anywhere in the world.

It is therefore no surprise that Google reported in 2015 that mobile searches have overtaken desktop queries. Furthermore, consumers are now using smartphones and tablets over desktops and laptops when engaging in online shopping. Given mums' love of the smartphone you can guess who is driving this.

In purchasing products or services online, mums want to reduce their level of risk. They look for free trials, money-back guarantees and free returns. While they enjoy the convenience of shopping online, they also don't want to pay extra for this, so they are attracted to Click & Collect or free shipping options.

Trend 6 – Supporting other mums

Mum loves to support other mums' businesses. She can empathise with the juggle of raising children as well as running a business, and believes a business mum understands her needs and the problems she faces better than other players in the market.

Mums are talented problem solvers and frequently launch a business to solve a problem they feel has been overlooked in the marketplace. That same problem is being experienced by loads of other mums so it is no surprise that mums love to support these endeavours.

Business owners who are also mums are more likely to provide the high level of service mums expect too. This is a major advantage for mums in business. At Bubbler we worked extensively with small business owners who also are mums and without question, sales conversions were higher when we profiled their business as being run by a mum who saw a need in the market and filled it.

There are a growing number of organisations supporting mums in business. These are typically led by mums themselves and exist to see mum-led businesses grow and prosper. They actively promote these businesses to their community.

MEET GABY

Gaby is a mum of three boys aged seven, 11 and 13 who juggles the demands of her boys' love of basketball, football and cricket with running a business. When she is not watching one of her boys at a sporting venue around Melbourne she is running her meal planning business, PlanBuyCook, which she co-founded with another mum at her children's school. Her business solves the daily 5 o'clock dilemma about what to cook for dinner. When she needs to outsource work or purchase equipment for her business, she will actively seek to purchase from other mum-led businesses. Gaby often asks other mums she knows for recommendations or posts in social media groups. She understands the pressures of growing a small business in Australia while raising children and wants to reward other mum-led businesses with her business.

MEET MANDY

Mandy is a 42-year-old sales director of a large multinational organisation and mother of two kids aged 13 and seven years. Despite work being an important and demanding part of her life, her family means everything to her and she likes to be present at all the major school events. This often means listening in to work conference calls while attending an athletics carnival, completing work after hours in order to be at a special school assembly or calling on a friend or family member to step in when she can't make it. She gets up early before the rest of the house to exercise and sometimes catches up on a TV show while on the cross trainer. She often has long periods in the car driving to and from the office and these periods provide her with a great opportunity to make appointments for the dentist, doctor, hairdresser or a catch-up with girlfriends on her Bluetooth-enabled phone. Not having much free time, she loves to do a spot of clothes shopping at the Sydney airport before boarding a plane to return to her home in Melbourne.

Trend 7 - Multitasking

Mum is increasingly multitasking. She cooks while checking emails, booking an appointment and assisting a child with their homework; she listens in to a work conference call while getting a load of laundry on. She spends an enormous amount of time each week caring for the other important people in her life. Multitasking is something she must do, rather than chooses to do, in order to meet all her commitments. Mum finds the juggle of life exhausting.

Mums have an increasingly short attention span and therefore their tolerance for timewasting 'noise' is lower than ever. This is why they demand clear messages that get to the point quickly. They want their time to be respected. Mums are multitasking during leisure time too. They are increasingly on their smartphones during the commercial breaks while watching TV, and this means less impact for TV advertisers.

Trend 8 – Information seeking

Mum is actively seeking information to make sure she is making the best decision, particularly for things concerning her family. She's researching online to support her buying decisions. Before she walks into a car showroom, she has researched the product, brand or company in detail. She is well down the path in her purchasing decision.

Mums have become very savvy, well-informed consumers. They will know what the competitor's alternative is, both price and availability, and will be happy to share this knowledge with you when negotiating the sale. Mums are turned off by sales representatives who underestimate their knowledge, research and their ability to understand technical information. Whatever you do, don't ever treat mum like she is stupid!

Pregnant mums are twice as likely to be seeking information online as other mums. This is reflective of the increased purchasing that a pregnant women undertakes in the preparation for a new baby. They want the absolute best for their new arrival and will invest considerable hours making sure they achieve this.

Breastfeeding and healthcare specialist Medela has conducted a survey of 4000 Australian mums who go online for parenting advice and support. It's not uncommon for a mum to be flicking through her phone seeking information while breastfeeding in the middle of the night.

MEET ANNA

Anna is a 35-year-old new mum of an eight-month-old baby. She's just gone back to work, returning on a part-time basis working in the accounts department for an electrical company. Still transitioning into life as a parent, Anna uses her smartphone to search medical information about health concerns she has about her daughter. When buying baby products, she seeks recommendations from her mother's group and other mothers she comes into contact with. Recently she was looking for nightclothes for her daughter where she would stay warm but wouldn't overheat. She asked her mother's group about sleeping bags for babies to find out if they were safe and to see if anyone was using a particular brand. With a recommendation from a couple of mums in the group, she then went online to check out the brand's website where she searched for product reviews. Content with her findings, she then made a purchase from a nearby store.

MEET SARAH

Sarah resides in Adelaide with her husband and two children aged one and three. Prior to having children, she worked fulltime negotiating mergers and acquisitions in a top-tier legal practice. Sarah loved nice clothes and homewares and often spent hours scrolling through magazines in her spare time selecting the right look for the season. After the birth of her first child, Sarah wanted more flexibility in her work arrangements and took a part-time role as a lawyer in a medium-sized company. With a reduced household income and a growing family to enjoy, Sarah doesn't have the time or inclination to invest in the latest trends and fashion like she previously did. Style is still very important to her but comfort and price have become the deciding factors. No longer is she interested in wearing ill-fitting, uncomfortable clothes in the name of fashion.

Trend 9 – Changing decision-making criteria

A UK study has shown that the criteria for making a purchase decision change dramatically once a woman becomes a mum. Price, comfort and safety become much more important. Price is a particularly sensitive area in the first twelve months of becoming a mum. This is often a period where a couple is relying on one salary and the kind of information mum is seeking out when researching for products or services reflects this. She is actively looking for value.

Trend 10 - Importance of storytelling

Mum is increasingly dissatisfied with pushy sales messages and is instead rewarding businesses who share stories and have more subtle sales messages. She wants to know a business's values.

An engaging story has been scientifically proven to connect with mum on an emotional level, establishing trust and forming a relationship. It is becoming increasingly important to mums that they know what a business values and how they treat their customers before they make their purchase decision. Mums are searching for these stories on a company website under 'About Us', and listening to other mums telling their story about a company on social media. Your sales pitch needs to represent your brand's story.

MEET MEGAN

Megan is a mum of four kids aged under 13 years including a set of seven-year-old twins. After a successful career working as a publicist in the arts industry both in Australia and overseas, she has recently started selling a very well-known home appliance that retails for more than $2000. Megan likes the flexibility of this part-time work and enjoys getting out and meeting new people. She loves the extra cash it brings into the household. Working part-time allows her to take her four children to their various sport and dance commitments. Megan knows the benefit of the product she sells only too well as she uses it every single day to cook for her children, two of whom are coeliac. At her product demonstrations, Megan shares stories about her experience cooking for her family with allergies. She also shares stories of real people who have bought the appliance from her, and how it has transformed the way they live. She finds the mums connect with actual real life stories rather than just hearing the product benefits. Sharing real life stories has enabled her to secure more sales.

KEY MISTAKES PEOPLE MAKE
WHEN SELLING TO MUMS

Despite the size and importance of mums as a consumer group, most businesses don't know how to successfully attract mums to their business and even fewer understand how to turn them into raving fans. In 2009 Forbes Magazine reported that a staggering 91 per cent of women felt misrepresented and misunderstood by advertisers. According to the Marketing to Mums survey, almost two thirds of Australian mums feel that advertisers don't understand them. These are alarming statistics for any business owner or marketer who targets Australian mums.

So how can this be? Well, for starters very few agencies are led by women and men tend to dominate the executive level of marketing in many businesses. This means it's probably more challenging to really tap into the nuances of mums and their communication styles and brand expectations – it's not where males naturally focus.

There is an enormous opportunity for businesses to delve deeper into the problems mums experience so that they can adjust their marketing efforts. Armed with a better understanding of mum, they can better solve her problems and significantly increase their sales and profit.

I have been studying mums over the past fifteen years and for every successful campaign aimed at mums, I see many more that fall short of the mark. Throughout almost five years running Bubbler and building a community of more than 90,000 in our social media (and winning an award for Best Social Media along the way), I have watched, listened and gathered rich learnings and insights about mums via our Facebook page. I want to share the top mistakes I see businesses make so you can avoid them, and I will be sharing what mums think advertisers need to do to connect with them, taken from our Marketing to Mums survey.

Mistake 1: Stereotyping

Stereotyping is the number one mistake mums believe advertisers make, according to the Marketing to Mums survey. Stereotyping your mum will significantly limit your ability to attract and retain your ideal target market. It will directly affect your sales conversions.

How many times are mums depicted as a size 8 woman, juggling her career in the boardroom with the needs of the kids? While I am sure those challenges are valid, Triumph – one of the world's leading manufacturers of lingerie and underwear – reports that 48 per cent of women in Australia and New Zealand are size 14 or above so this stereotype immediately isolates your brand from the very person you are trying to attract.

In a massive study undertaken in 2014 by advertising giant Saatchi & Saatchi in conjunction with popular UK parenting site Mumsnet, they found that only 19 per cent of UK mums have ever seen a woman in an ad

Don't think that because we are mums we want ugly dressing gowns, fluffy slippers, cookware or cleaning appliances. We like being self-sufficient. We will use tools, fix broken things. We are not afraid of getting dirty. We are not just mums, we are modern women.

#inmumswords

that they can actually identify with. Furthermore, they found stereotyping of the perfect mum was a real turn-off with 74 per cent of respondents claiming they weren't aspiring to mothering perfection anyway.

Stereotyping will make you appear disingenuous. You might think you are appealing to the aspirational mum, but more often than not you will just turn her away from your brand. She can't relate.

Mistake 2: Treating mums like they are all the same

Not all mums are the same. Many businesses target 'mums' in general, afraid to niche for fear of limiting their market. They attempt to appeal to all types of mums rather than really understanding the key issues faced by their Ideal Mum customer. (See page 70 for more about your Ideal Mum.) As a result, they connect with very few mums and wonder why sales aren't coming in.

From the Marketing to Mums survey results, we identified that mums think that treating them as if they

Don't try and appeal to
the masses. Know who your
audience is and then speak to
them as opposed to thinking
all mums think and worry
about the same thing.

#inmumswords

are all the same is the second biggest mistake advertisers make when trying to connect with them. Mums want to be recognised as women first, mothers second and they want their differences understood and reflected in the way a business interacts with them.

Mistake 3: Pushing for a sale

It is no wonder mum is exhausted! Apparently the volume of marketing messages we receive each day has increased tenfold since the 1970s, and given her purchasing power, she is being targeted constantly – in the wrong way.

Mums are increasingly rejecting corporate sales messages and relying on mum-to-mum recommendations. They don't want pushy sales strategies. So often, I see marketers using a push strategy to sell their brand's features and benefits when they could increase their return on investment significantly by creating an environment where they can facilitate a mum-to-mum conversation with their brand. Nothing is more powerful and I am constantly amazed by the number of brands out there content to just push their wares. It is essential that marketers find innovative ways to utilise their best brand advocates as part of their marketing strategy.

Make the ad less pushy. I get suspicious that it's not a good product when it's all salesy.

#inmumswords

Mistake 4: Not being real

Mums often feel a disconnect between advertising and their reality. They feel their lives are being trivialised and incorrectly portrayed and mums will dismiss your message if you don't represent them correctly. They want an honest portrayal and real communication. Be real. Authenticity is key.

Mums want marketers to stop portraying perfect lives with mothers who have got it all together because it is just not the life that they are living, and it's not one they aspire to either. The perfectly dressed mum in clean ironed trousers, heels and a jacket wheeling a pram with a coffee in one hand is not most mums' reality. Most women really dislike the 'perfect mum' image being used as they simply cannot relate to it. Many mums consider it to be a major achievement that they are up, have clothes on (even if they don't match) and have managed to get out of the house with their child and are tending to that child's needs.

Mums aren't striving for perfection. They are striving to make their lives easier so by failing to keep it real you are doing a gross disservice to your brand and limiting your opportunity to create strong brand relationships and increase your sales.

By not depicting the complexity of mum's life and thereby simplifying her, you ostracise her. It fuels her desire to rely on more mum-to-mum recommendations where she can trust the quality information provided to her. By not being real you cannot build trust and without trust you cannot achieve loyalty.

Don't pay celebs for advertising, use real people who want to be heard. Celebrities earn enough money and we resent the fact that they are getting paid more to 'like' a product. Use real people who really like and use the product. It's not rocket science!

#inmumswords

Mistake 5: Failing to build a relationship first

Too often we see marketers going in for the hard sell before they even develop a relationship with mums. As James Tuckerman, founder of Anthill Online, Australia's largest online community for entrepreneurs, would say, marketers are attempting to hit on them without even taking them out for a drink. There needs to be a courting period.

Mums want to get to know your brand and what your business stands for. Social media provides a great opportunity to build a relationship but many businesses are failing to care about building a strong relationship before starting to sell. As a result, they do not have a connection with their Ideal Mum. They miss key insights about her problems so there are no opportunities to improve upon their product or to better service her needs. Without a relationship there is unlikely to be any brand loyalty. It places ongoing sales in jeopardy.

Mistake 6: Lack of social support

All businesses have the opportunity to connect with their customers via social media yet I am constantly amazed by the number of brands and businesses who do not do this. They don't have a social media presence, let alone a strong social media strategy.

In Australia only 48 per cent of small and 54 per cent of medium businesses have a social media presence, according to the Sensis Social Media Report of 2016.

This is growing, however I don't believe it's fast enough. The figures improve for large businesses with 79 per cent connecting via social media. The report also found that in the past twelve months Australians spent an additional four hours each week on social media making it an impressive 12.5 hours each week engaged in social media. Investment in social media is relatively low, less than 14 per cent of total marketing budget.

Listen to what mums are saying! Often the SAHMs have researched and tested products or items extensively. Social media has a huge impact on what we spend our dollars on as mums get savvier!

#inmumswords

I think the reliance on social media is significantly more important in businesses that target mums and by failing to invest in social media, you are missing key insights about mums and the chance to develop a stronger relationship. It is costing you sales and limits repeat business. This applies whether you are a service- or product-based business. It applies to bricks-and-mortar stores just as much as online businesses. Neglecting social media assets is a key mistake for any business targeting mums.

Mistake 7: Treating mums as stupid

Mums want you to respect their intelligence and understand that they are capable of processing technical information. They hate it when you simplify your marketing message and dumb it down. They find it patronising. In the Marketing to Mums survey, they were vocal about the fact that advertisers often treated them like they'd lost their brain with the birth of a baby.

What is even worse is when businesses invest their marketing budget into targeting the wrong market. Women are the key decision makers when it comes to the purchase of cars and electronics and yet how many ads can you recall that target them? By failing to acknowledge that mums are informed powerful consumers you are significantly limiting your sales conversions.

Nowhere is this more obvious than in the automotive industry. Juliet Potter, founder of AutoChic.com.au told me that 'women purchase 70 per cent of all new vehicles in Australia and make the final decision in 85 per cent of all new car purchases'. Yet when women walk into a showroom they are typically greeted by a male sales representative. They are rarely offered a test drive and when they wish to talk to a sales rep about a car model they are likely to be greeted with what colour choice they might make as opposed to the fuel economy or safety and performance features. In short, the automotive industry patronises mums and treats them like they are stupid.

I may appear with vomit on my shoulder, hair unbrushed and distracted by the screaming toddler – but my mind is just as sharp, maybe sharper, than when I was in corporate. So sell to me accordingly. Picture me in a suit, if it helps.

#inmumswords

It is not surprising that mums do not enjoy the process of buying a new vehicle. Imagine the difference if companies diverted their marketing spend to connect with mums and employed female sales representatives in each branch. Imagine the return on that marketing investment.

Mistake 8: Offering no value

Mums can be very savvy shoppers. Many have made the transition from double-income-no-kids to one or one-and-a-half incomes with dependants. There is an increasing need to find value and businesses need to understand what is actually valued as this might not necessarily be price.

The critical mistake being made here is that many businesses fail to demonstrate their value. This is typically because they don't have a deep understanding of their Ideal Mum and fail to understand how she assesses value. I've had businesses come to me telling me that they want us to create a campaign around X; when we review the material, we know that women want to know about Y. How? We've taken nearly five years of experience working with hundreds of brands and growing a community of 150,000-plus mums around the country. We understand mums. Your job is to have a depth of awareness about what she values.

Mistake 9: Lack of third party endorsement

Mums are information seeking and looking for reviews and recommendations to solve their problems, so why do businesses fail to make these easily available for them? The absence of genuine website testimonials, social media reviews and recommendations is a key mistake I see businesses make all the time. Without access to this information, mum is likely to look elsewhere and you miss a potential sale. The good news is that this is very simple to correct and costs nothing, and will assist your mum on the path to purchase.

Encouraging word of mouth or reviews. It is the biggest reason I buy what I buy.

#inmumswords

part 2

8 PILLARS
OF SUCCESS

Throughout my career, I've been involved in marketing or selling products targeted at mums. I've worked with over a hundred businesses of all sizes, across diverse industries. But it wasn't until I became a mum myself – and was therefore on the receiving end of the way brands were marketed to mothers – that I could see that mums were misunderstood and their needs and behaviours misinterpreted. The marketing mistakes were plentiful.

I became really interested in the ways businesses could increase their sales conversions to mums, and how I could help them do that. I've seen many businesses fail because they weren't implementing effective strategies in this area. If marketers got this right, I recognised it would deliver mums more meaningful content and reduce the amount of noise they'd need to filter each day. They'd be able to find solutions to problems faster and purchasing would become a much better experience than it is now – a win for both mums and businesses.

There are key differences between men and women when it comes to purchase decision-making. Mums are astute, sophisticated shoppers who are prepared to invest time in the hope of discovering the best solution for their needs. A woman's criteria for purchasing are likely to be wider than a man's. She is more likely to visit multiple stores, both online and bricks-and-mortar, to find the ultimate solution. Men, in comparison, are task-oriented shoppers who just want to get the job done and get out of there in as little time as possible. I highly recommend you watch Mark Gungor's 'Tale of Two Brains'. It is an entertaining and informative presentation on how gender impacts thinking which is available on YouTube.

Tapping into a mum's journey can be challenging for many businesses, so I have developed an eight-step plan that identifies the key ingredients to successfully market your product or service to mums. I call it the 8 Pillars of Success and believe that if you follow this framework you will:

→ Have a greater understanding of your target audience
→ Have the tools to develop and share your own brand story
→ Understand your point of difference to assist you to position your brand in your industry
→ Ensure you can delight mums with your customer experience

→ Understand simple low-cost methods to build your email list

→ Learn how to attract and secure marketing partnerships

→ Know how to harness the power of social media

→ Discover low-cost ways to promote your business

By implementing the above pillars I am confident that you will increase your sales. In fact, before you commence this work , I challenge you to record your sales now and 12 months after implementing changes from my framework. I expect you will be pleasantly surprised at how small tweaks to the way you do things can result in big changes to your sales outcomes.

STEP 1: UNDERSTAND YOUR IDEAL MUM

To avoid some of the marketing pitfalls when selling to mum, first you need to understand her. It's no longer satisfactory to say that your business focuses on 'mums'. The market segment is simply too wide and you will struggle to appeal to all mums and end up relating to very few and

Stop using sexist stereotypes to promote your brands. I stop using products promoted this way (and I am running out of products to buy).

#inmumswords

wondering why your business isn't growing. Do not be afraid to niche. In short, you need to identify your ideal customer. We'll refer to her as your Ideal Mum. As Glen Carlson, the co-founder of Dent®, an award-winning training organisation helping entrepreneurs and leaders to stand up and scale up, says, you need to understand your Ideal Mum like your best friend because by having knowledge around her problems, motivations, desires and needs you will be able to form a better relationship and create better solutions for her. This will deliver you greater sales and loyal customers.

Firstly you really need to understand her values. Not just her conscious but her *unconscious* values. It has been reported that 90 per cent of the purchase decision has already been made in the unconscious. This is staggering and highlights the importance of delving deep into the mind of your Ideal Mum to discover why she does what she does. The 'why' is important because her past behaviour is likely to provide you with some key learnings into her potential future behaviour.

My message here is that before you can even start to think about preparing your marketing strategy you need to understand more about your Ideal Mum. What kind of mum is she? Where does she spend her time? What are her key problems? Don't neglect the psychographic profile of your mum audience. Understanding who she is really is vital if you are going to get her attention.

IDEAL MUM AVATAR

At Bubbler, I got to know our Ideal Mum very well after almost five years in business, by listening to her on our Facebook page, by undertaking surveys and reviewing her purchase data. So who is she?

→ She is aged 25–44 years with kids aged under 12 years.

→ She is either a stay-at-home mum or working part-time.

→ She is married and lives in a house located 12–50 kilometres from a major city.

→ She is part of a two-car family.

→ Her household income has been reduced dramatically since having children.

→ She is looking to save money.

→ She puts her kids first always and doesn't want them to miss out on all the fun activities in life.

→ She is active in her local community and wants to contribute to fundraising efforts at her local playgroup or primary school but her weekly budget is under pressure.

→ She volunteers often but is conflicted that she cannot contribute more to her children's school or playgroup.

→ She doesn't get out with her girlfriends as much as she'd like so loves unique experiences where she can make a girls' night out.

→ She is looking for new things to do to get her out of the house and remove her feeling of isolation.

→ She has some discretionary income and enjoys being able to try new things but not at full price, in effect reducing her perceived risk in case she doesn't like it.

→ She is always receptive to products that improve her life or the life of her family.

→ She is trying to be the best mum she can and worries about her children's eating.

→ She finds cooking a bit monotonous and she loves having someone provide her with some inspiration for cooking for the family.

→ She enjoys having a laugh at herself and socialising with other like-minded mums.

→ Her children are more likely to attend a public rather than a private school.

→ She is probably existing on reduced sleep as she is the primary care-giver and may be up in the night attending to children.

→ Community is really important to her and she seeks to belong.

→ She is really active on social media. In fact, it is the first thing she does in the morning, with quick checks through the day and later returning to 'socialise from the couch' where she will watch television and surf the net and talk with friends on social media.

→ She is comfortable with online shopping having engaged in it many times before and she loves the convenience of not having to take the kids with her.

→ She loves her smartphone which is never far from her as she likes to get out and about.

→ The three biggest problems facing her are: lack of money, lack of time and isolation.

→ She will act on a mum recommendation and prefers more subtle forms of advertising.

→ Subconsciously she worries about whether she is a good parent, if her kids are going to turn out alright, if her child is being bullied, whether they can pay the mortgage, when they'll need to upgrade the car or renovate the house.

→ She wants to feel carefree and youthful so that she can get out and play with her kids.

CASE STUDY

Recently I spoke to a small business owner who was running a school holiday program for girls aged 11–17 years. She was charging $119 for a one-day program and wasn't getting the registrations she expected. I asked her a series of questions about her Ideal Mum to gain a better understanding of what the problem was. Within ten minutes, we established that her pricing policy did not reflect her ideal client. She had created her marketing campaign around characteristics of a mum who was not her ideal client. The following morning she put together a picture of her ideal client including both demographic and psychographic information. She immediately reduced her price to reflect her ideal customer which had an immediate impact on her sign-ups. Three clients immediately booked in. You need to narrow down the characteristics of your Ideal Mum – by really understanding these characteristics you can create a strategy to attract this client to your business.

KNOW YOUR IDEAL MUM: Without a clear understanding of who she is, you are lost and falling into the trap of appealing to no one.

I am a big advocate for conducting primary research to determine just who your Ideal Mum is. SurveyMonkey is a cost-effective survey software program which can be used to uncover insights about your customer. I invest considerable time at this first stage as it determines the success of your marketing strategy. A poorly identified Ideal Mum will result in poor results for your marketing efforts. Don't rush this step.

All your marketing efforts should be directly at your Ideal Mum. Do not worry if you feel too niched. The more focused the niche, the greater your impact. You will also attract others on the borders of the niche but without a clearly defined niche there is no point investing any marketing dollars at all.

I've shared the Bubbler Ideal Mum avatar with you on page 72 so you can get a sense of the depth of knowledge you need to have around your Ideal Mum. The important parts of our Bubbler avatar are the lifestyle factors which motivate her. We understand that she comes to our website to save money, find new things and places to discover, and to help her local community. These reasons are aligned with her values.

The following checklist is a selection of the questions you should be asking yourself about your Ideal Mum. It's by no means exhaustive but I want you to spend at least 30 minutes writing down as much as you can about your Ideal Mum. If you are really unsure who she is, review your sales and see who is consistently buying from you. Ask to speak with this customer and delve into why she purchases from you and get an understanding of her life – her challenges and joys. Essentially, you're looking for what makes her act the way she does. You can also map out where your existing customers live.

Once you understand who your Ideal Mum is, give her a name and think about what she looks like. Look for a photo that represents her graphically. It was once suggested to me that I pin my avatar up in the office for all my staff to see. I encourage you to do the same. If you are a solo operator, pin the avatar graphic somewhere you will see it all day long. Any decision made in your business needs to consider your Ideal Mum so it makes sense to have her top of mind visually in your office.

We went a step further in Bubbler to give her a name: Julie. She featured on our office door and we were constantly reminded about who we were trying to connect with. She was our ideal advertising client.

Allocate a portion of each day to talking and engaging with your Ideal Mum. Yes, every day. It will enable you to stay focused on her in all your business processes. It will provide you with greater insights into her problems and the more important subtle changes she experiences. Being able to pick up on these subtle changes will allow you to better tailor your business to providing her with the perfect solution. The greater your desire to build relationships with your Ideal Mum and grow your business, the greater the time you should allocate. Social media is a great place to do this daily check-in on your Ideal Mum.

 **CHECKLIST**

- ○ Age range?
- ○ Does she have dependent children living at home?
- ○ How many children does she have?
- ○ How old are her children?
- ○ Does she have a partner?
- ○ Where does she live?
- ○ What is her household income?
- ○ Is she the primary carer of her children?
- ○ Does she work? Part-time? Fulltime?
- ○ What does she like to do?
- ○ What doesn't she like to do?
- ○ Where does she go in her typical day?
- ○ Does she do a weekly shop or a bit each day?
- ○ How often does she use social media?
- ○ What's her favourite time to go on social media?
- ○ What is her favourite social media platform?
- ○ What media does she watch, listen to or read?
- ○ What are her hopes and aspirations?
- ○ What does she worry about?
- ○ What is she passionate about?
- ○ What are the biggest problems she faces?
- ○ What does she value?
- ○ Where does she holiday?
- ○ What are her hobbies?
- ○ What does she aspire to do?

Now start thinking about how well you know your Ideal Mum and whether your attempts to engage really target her. I often see clients who do actually have a good sense of their Ideal Mum but their marketing is not directed at this person. There are clear disconnects. Now is the time to identify your Ideal Mum and see if your existing marketing strategy aligns. If it doesn't, make the tweaks and reap the rewards. Simple changes can unlock more sales.

> **ACTION**
> Your first task is to create an avatar that represents your Ideal Mum. Give her a name and start to describe her, answering the questions on the checklist.

STEP 2: BUILD YOUR BRAND

A strong brand, clearly communicated, will increase your sales conversions. Branding is highly underrated. While I understand that there can be financial constraints, it is important that you don't focus exclusively on short-term conversions. It will erode the long-term sustainability of your business.

The key objective of this section is to ensure that you can articulate what your brand represents, what problem you solve for your Ideal Mum and whether this is in alignment with your marketing efforts. We are going to uncover any holes in your brand and develop your brand story so that it is aligned with what your Ideal Mum values, so your customers can become loyal fans.

Be more realistic in your portrayal of mums. We aren't all chino-wearing blonde ladies with perfect kids and a border collie. Being a mum is bloody hard work and we deserve to be respected for that.

#inmumswords

What do you stand for?

What does your business stand for? What is the key problem you solve for your Ideal Mum? Is it clear on your website and promotional materials? If I stumbled across your page on Facebook, would I understand what problem you solve?

People don't buy what you sell. They buy why you sell it.

Simon Sinek

BUBBLER stands for quality living on a limited budget. Bubbler seeks to empower women, provide value, contribute to society and offer quality service.

→ Empowering women – supporting female business owners.

→ Value – assisting mums to save money by finding value-for-money shopping offers.

→ Social responsibility – giving back 5% of voucher sales to approved primary schools and playgroups.

→ Quality of service – focusing on above average customer service.

The words I would use to describe the Bubbler brand are accessible, unique, fun and real. We are not appealing to aspirational women or the elite socialites. We are about the mum in the suburbs who is doing a huge and often overwhelming job of caring for the family. Remember, she powers the spending of our nation. We work to portray mum as realistically as possible. We reflect the fun and unique aspect of our brand through the content and shopping offers we present to our community of mums. Many of our sales are exclusive and we work hard to seek out unusual activities to provide unique and fun events for mums and families. Mums have a high expectation of customer service in comparison to men so it's important that we focus on above average customer service.

PROBLEM SOLVED: Our Ideal Mum can stretch her household budget further while benefitting her community, and that is done through relevant savvy shopping offers. We provide her with feel-good shopping.

My consulting business, **MARKETING TO MUMS**, specialises in helping businesses sell more to Australia's most powerful consumer, mums. My business stands for respecting mums, driving social change and growing businesses.

→ Mums: We want mums to not be bombarded with lame, irrelevant sales messages all day long.

→ Social change: We know mums are highly undervalued by most sectors of business. We want to be their advocates in order to change the way they are viewed and valued by business.

→ Disruption: As the only consultancy specialising in mums we want to provide leading research into Australian mums in order to bust myths about who they are.

→ Growth: We want to help businesses increase their sales and profit through meaningful relationships and communications with mums.

PROBLEM SOLVED: Businesses don't know Australian mums as well as they should. Using primary research into the behaviour and opinions of mums, Marketing to Mums demystifies this powerful market sector so that businesses can increase return on investment in their marketing spend.

ACTION

Take 20–30 minutes out of your day. Think again about your Ideal Mum. Now pretend you are starting your business from scratch, and write down what your brand would stand for and what adjectives you might use to describe your brand. Reflect on how this fits with your Ideal Mum and what she values.

If you identify a disconnect between your Ideal Mum and your brand story, congratulations! You now have the perfect opportunity to change things. Aligning your brand with your Ideal Mum should deliver great results within months as long as you effectively communicate and promote your changes. If your business can afford it, I would recommend getting a marketing consultant at this point, to review and alter your brand attributes so that they appeal to your mum but still feel authentically 'you'. If finances are limited, do this yourself and then seek feedback in any business networks you operate within to check that the realignment of your brand makes sense. There are lots of very helpful business groups online and you could tap into their collective mind too.

If you are still unsure about whether your brand is in alignment, get on the phone and talk with some of your Ideal Mums and get their opinions. Mums love to share their feedback.

Brand language

Now you understand your Ideal Mum and what your brand stands for, is the language you use appropriate? When I started Bubbler I had just spent fifteen years in the corporate arena and my communication style was rather businesslike, while my Ideal Mum wanted a more conversational style. Initially I was unaware I was making this mistake but thankfully one of my business partners provided me with this constructive feedback. It took some practice but I was able to drop my corporate language. Examine the language you are using to talk to your Ideal Mum, paying attention to your tone or 'voice'.

If your language is not in keeping with your Ideal Mum, it creates an immediate disconnect. It leads to confusion around what your brand is about and a confused customer will never make a purchase.

A key point to make here is that 'conversational' does not mean 'dumbed down'. Too often I see businesses dumbing down their language because they presume mums are not able to understand it. Too often, a business will ostracise a mum by not speaking to her correctly. I encourage you to get active on social media and watch how your Ideal Mum interacts and the language she uses to establish what language your business should be using.

LOOK AT THIS

MULBERRY is a premium accessory brand in the UK. One of the funniest advertisements I've seen in a while was their 2014 campaign, aimed at driving Christmas sales. In the TV commercial a mother is being presented with her gifts. Her daughter gives her a portrait she has painted of her mum. Mum smiles, appreciative. Then the woman's mother presents her with a puppy. Her partner tops that with a unicorn, appearing at the window. The competitive gift-giving gets sillier as the ad progresses, with each wanting to outdo the other. We then see a very meek grandmother present her gift. Mum opens the package and absolutely loses it with excitement. Suddenly, she has gone from a very contained upper-class mum to a more relatable mum as she jumps up, squeals with delight and uses language that is totally out of kilter with her posh surrounds. She absolutely and genuinely loves the gift. Granny has trumped them all by giving a Mulberry handbag. The ad ends with the hashtag #WinChristmas – perfectly appealing to mums who love social media for all the beautiful things you can capture.

Search for the ad on YouTube under #WinChristmas. It's well worth the few minutes.

ACTION

Think about your Ideal Mum again. Reflect on the language you use on your website, when you or your staff speak with customers, and in your marketing materials. List three improvements you could make in your brand language and action them. Call a team meeting and share it. Your team needs to understand and communicate your brand too.

Your brand story

Your brand story is one of the most compelling pieces you can share with your Ideal Mum. Authentically describing what drove you to start your business, what you are trying to achieve and how you want to make the life of a mum easier will speak volumes. Well executed, it will build a bond with your mum, deepen the relationship and ultimately assist you to sell more of your product or service.

So many times I come across brands led by amazing people who are attempting to display their business as being much bigger than it is, thinking their Ideal Mum will have greater confidence in buying from them. They use words like 'we' and 'us' rather than 'I' and 'me'. Don't underestimate the power of being yourself and sharing your story.

Women business owners, please take note as you are so often the ones who are content to be behind the scenes. You are doing a great disservice to your business. Your Ideal Mum wants to know about you, what motivated you to start your business, and they want to share your ups and downs too. Your 'why' is so important for your Ideal Mum to understand. Let them be part of your journey as mums are increasingly wanting to feel a part of a brand's community.

CASE STUDY

MY LIL POUCH sells reusable food pouches that enable people to save money and guarantee the quality of food they are giving their kids while out and about. The founder, Sarah Hansen, came to me in 2014 with the simple aim of wanting to increase sales. Sarah is a mum of two sets of twins yet very few of her customers knew this about her. We created a compelling offer to promote My Lil Pouch to the Bubbler community and the key focus of the entire campaign was sharing Sarah's story. This pushed Sarah out of her comfort zone. She was not keen to share her story and it was some days before I could convince her to try this strategy. She eventually agreed and provided a photograph of her in hospital with her new twins, older twins and husband.

We wanted mums to connect with Sarah and her juggle of raising four children – twins no less. The Facebook post alone sent so much traffic to her website we set a new record for best daily visits. She could inspire other mums to start a business themselves and they wanted to support her business. They felt a connection with her. Sarah now regularly shares her story when promoting her business.

COMMUNICATE YOUR BRAND: The reusable food pouches allow mums on the run to feed their kids healthy food. Mums identify with Sarah's personal story which gives the product credibility.

LUCAS LOVES CARS is a great example of a strong brand story, developed by Helle Warming. Helle started her business in 2012 after the birth of her son Lucas who was crazy about cars and anything that moved. She identified a gap in the marketplace for an online toy and gift retailer who exclusively catered for the car- and train-loving child by providing quality wooden vehicles, trains and aircraft. Her brand story is incorporated into her trading name and she brings it to life on her website in a mum-to-mum style conversational manner. She shares stories about her car-obsessed son along with family pictures and Lucas's drawings. Helle understands the importance of Lucas being part of her brand and he often features in videos demonstrating how to use or enjoy some of her products on her Facebook page. By sharing her brand story, she allows her Ideal Mum to get to know her and understand what motivated her to start her business.

COMMUNICATE YOUR BRAND: Helle understands how hard it can be for busy mums to find quality specialist toys and used her son's story to connect with others in her position.

ACTION

Are you successfully communicating your brand story? Does your Ideal Mum understand why you are in business and what your business values are? If you haven't already seen it, I recommend watching Simon Sinek's TED talk, 'Start with Why'.

Sit down and write your brand story. If you find it easier, take a walk around the block and audio record these details into your phone. Answer these questions: why did you start, what motivates you, what are you passionate about delivering to your Ideal Mum, how can you make their life easier. Sit on it for a day or two, before refining it. Then record it. This can be as simple as doing it on your iPhone, or go to a studio, but record it. You might have to do it a few times, but when you're happy with it, upload it to your social media channels and get it up on your website.

Review the About Us/Our Story/My Story section of your website. Is your story well reflected? If you don't have an 'About Us' page set one up immediately. Besides your landing page, this is the most trafficked page on your website.

Brand touch points

Marketing expert Dr Jeffrey Lant states that your brand needs to contact or 'touch' a potential purchaser seven times within an 18-month period to create a sale. The true number of touch points required, I believe, depends greatly on the type of product or service you have, its price, quality and other variables, but I do think that Lant's seven-touch rule is a great yardstick. Therefore it is critical that you establish how your Ideal Mum spends her time, where she goes and when she is online in order to progress her along the path to purchase from you.

By having a clear understanding of your Ideal Mum you are in a better position to create these touch points and provide her with information that highlights she has a need for your product. You'll create awareness around your brand and enable her to make the transaction. You'll encourage loyalty with a post-purchase experience to assist her on a path to repeat purchase or endorsement to other potential purchasers. Your consideration around touch points should not be just to make the sale but to develop a relationship with your Ideal Mum, converting her into a raving fan where she freely advocates for your brand, effectively becoming a touch point herself.

Put time into getting to know me, my circumstances and my wants – I am not just a sales commission. I actually matter.

#inmumswords

✔ **CHECKLIST**

Potential brand touch points include:

- ○ Your website
- ○ Your logo
- ○ Your speaking engagements, workshops or appearances at events
- ○ Reading your blog or an article you have written on a third party platform
- ○ Your social media
- ○ Advertising
- ○ Joint marketing partnerships
- ○ Public relations initiatives
- ○ Your newsletter
- ○ Interviews, podcasts, webinars
- ○ Social influencers talking about your product or service
- ○ Brand ambassadors
- ○ Your branded van or car on the road
- ○ Signage outside your office
- ○ The appearance of you and your staff
- ○ Quality of your presentations to prospects
- ○ Trade shows
- ○ Review sites
- ○ Employees who work for you
- ○ What other mums are saying about your business both offline and online

> **ACTION**
> Now that you have clearly identified your Ideal Mum,
> list all the possible brand touch points your Ideal Mum
> could experience. Review these brand touches and
> identify if they are all reflective of your brand values and
> brand story. If not, make adjustments.

Brand consistency

Now that you have a clear idea of who your Ideal Mum is, and have developed your brand story and established your business's touch points, you need to ensure brand consistency. What do I mean by that? Well, you need to ensure that everything you do and say reflects your brand on an ongoing basis.

At a marketing level this might mean making sure your brand colours, logo and tagline are used on all communications. It could include ensuring your brand message is repeated throughout your marketing collateral. But brand consistency goes well beyond your marketing materials – it really is about what you do and say.

In the case of Lucas Loves Cars (see Case Study on page 88), Helle involves Lucas in her product demonstrations, making videos showing how much fun can be derived from playing with a particular toy or book which is available for sale on her website.

In my own business, the Bubbler brand is about superior service so we ensure that we have processes in place within our business for responding promptly to customer enquiries. This extends to our merchant clients also, with suppliers being paid within 48 hours of submitting their invoices. This is part of ensuring that we are consistently delivering upon our brand values.

ACTION
Take a half-hour and review the processes and systems within your business. Do they reinforce your brand attributes? Can you integrate more of your brand story into other elements of your business?

Building trust

In the majority of cases, women take longer to make a purchase decision than men. We are not trying to be difficult, it is just how we are wired! Women like to research longer and really consider their options as they seek to arrive at the perfect solution to their problem. We are seeing a decline in brand loyalty with mums increasingly trusting the views of other mums over a business sales message. This presents a great challenge to business owners and marketers. To protect the long-term sustainability of your business, you need to work very hard to gain mum's trust. This won't be easy; however,

Ratings and reviews count. A lot of mums spend more time researching a product than buying.

#inmumswords

once you've achieved this, you are likely to have a raving fan who will share your business with all the mums they meet so it is incredibly worthwhile. Long before your Ideal Mum makes a purchase, she needs to have established a bond and a degree of trust in your business so you need to show empathy towards her.

LOOK AT THIS

#SHARETHELOAD is a very successful overseas campaign run by a laundry powder brand. It's a powerful advertisement which shows an elderly Indian father silently apologising for all the mistakes he made by reinforcing gender in parenting his now-adult daughter. He now feels responsible for the fact that she does all the laundry in the household as well as her work outside the home. The ad shows great empathy towards the mum, as her father learns to use the washing machine. It is great to see a corporate brand supporting social change by sharing the message that men should help with household chores and that we should stop perpetuating it as women's work. The campaign was very well received and went viral on social media, shared by mums around the world.

Your brand story is one of the most powerful ways you can create rapport with your Ideal Mum and start to build trust. Every few months I used to do a post on the Bubbler Facebook page where I welcomed new fans, introduced myself, shared a picture of myself and shared why I started my business. It was written for new people who had joined our community and was designed to humanise my business and position it as a personalised business, led by a mum for other mums. I supported it by promoting our reviews, sharing testimonials and my own experiences with particular clients.

ACTION
Search #ShareTheLoad on YouTube and watch the advertisement. Now reflect on how you might be able to show empathy towards your Ideal Mum. Create a welcome video or post for new, prospective and existing customers introducing yourself, what your business mission is and how you can make your Ideal Mum's life easier. Update and share this periodically with your community.

STEP 3: POSITION YOUR BUSINESS

By now you understand your Ideal Mum, you've written your brand story using appropriate language to communicate with your tribe, and you know your business touch points. Next you need to position your business to attract your Ideal Mum. A strong market position can attract more customers,

> Stop cookie cutting mums and stereotyping us as 50s housewives. We're busines women, we're engaged, we're savvy, we compare and shop around.
>
> **#inmumswords**

potentially reducing your marketing investment. It can assist you to create an attraction strategy where your Ideal Mum seeks you out.

In researching this book, I spoke with many small business owners who struggle with market positioning. Many can't articulate how their business is positioned in the market and spoke of increasing competition and finding business tougher and tougher, with lots of new players entering the market. They find themselves resorting to battling it out over price, competing with much larger businesses who would run the same products or services as a loss leader. They feel they are squeezing their profits because they need to reduce the price of their goods to stay competitive. It's a vicious cycle placing huge pressure on their cash flow.

I want to show you an easier way. Yes, you can position

your business as the cheapest, however I don't believe that is sustainable for most small businesses as they are often competing with larger organisations with deeper pockets. You need to position your business on factors other than price.

Firstly, think about your business from your Ideal Mum's point of view. In an increasingly competitive world where mums are such a sought-after consumer group, she is being smashed with sales messages all day long. She can find it overwhelming. Your business needs to understand not only how your product or service is better or different from everything else out there but, more importantly, how it makes your Ideal Mum's life easier.

Ask yourself, what makes you unique or different? Many businesses struggle with this question, unsure why their customers keep coming back. It is our differences which allow us to stand out from the pack and these need to be amplified.

Mums are more than one market. Know which market the mum you want is in.

#inmumswords

If you feel unsure about what makes your business unique, I've put together some questions to prompt you. You need to establish what makes you better and different and, more importantly, why your Ideal Mum should care. How do you make her life easier?

✔ CHECKLIST

- ○ Can you deliver a really personalised service (for example, with a handwritten note accompanying each order)?
- ○ Is your packaging or product delivery system unique?
- ○ Do you have a money-back guarantee?
- ○ Do you offer exceptional quality?
- ○ Do you contribute to a cause that is important to your Ideal Mum?
- ○ Is your product range unique?
- ○ Do you have the fastest turnaround on delivery or services, faster than anyone else in your category?
- ○ Do you have international experience?
- ○ What do you do that your competitors don't?

ACTION

Write down all the things that make your business better or different from the competition. Next to each point, determine if and how this makes your Ideal Mum's life easier. If you don't offer anything unique or your product doesn't make your Ideal Mum's life easier in some way, then I suggest you address this now and work out how your product or service could deliver an improved experience that better meets her needs.

CASE STUDY

TOOSH COOSH is a moulded portable booster seat that helps to eliminate the wriggling toddler from the dinner table. It's a mum invention designed here in Australia by Joanne Turner. I have worked with Toosh Coosh on multiple campaigns, each time focusing on the fact that the product has been invented by a mum, and that its unique moulded nature makes life easier around mealtimes. We have successfully sold more than 900 units of old packaged stock over a six-month period and received amazing feedback from mums around the country.

POSITION YOUR BRAND: This is a 'family mealtime revolution' that addresses the dinnertime nightmare faced by many mums. All the communication around the product's function is about avoiding food on the floor, wriggling kids, and general kid-related stress.

Brand positioning methodology

Once you are clear about what makes your business better and different, you need to do an industry analysis. This will help you understand where you are right now, meaning how your brand is already perceived. Once you understand where *you* are currently positioned, you can look at how your competitors are positioned.

There are three simple stages you can work through:

1. Where are you now?

If you are unsure of how you are currently positioned, ask your frequent customers. Send out a survey or conduct personalised interviews to find out why they keep coming back. You want to know what they think when they think about your brand. What emotions are associated with your brand? Get two pieces of butcher paper and on one start jotting down all their emotions that come to mind when your brand is mentioned, and on another list down all the reasons they say they come back to your business.

2. Where are your competitors?

Now it's time to look at the competition and establish how they are positioning their business. Examine their website, get in their stores, look at their social media and work out how they are wanting to be perceived. Check their reviews to see how they are perceived as this can also highlight competitor shortcomings. To me, this is a step many small business owners don't spend enough time on. As a result, they completely miss out on opportunities to position their business where a competitor is not.

3. Revisit your Ideal Mum

I think it's important to revisit your Ideal Mum at this time. Remind yourself what factors are important in her making a decision to purchase your product or service. Check to see if there are one or more factors that are not currently being met by competitors or your business.

ACTION

Work through the three stages, and identify if there are gaps available in the market that fit with your brand and your Ideal Mum and determine your desired market position.

CASE STUDY

When I was researching **BUBBLER** using brand positioning methodology it very quickly became evident that there was a gap in the marketplace. Not only was there a perception of poor customer service within the group buying industry generally, there was no dedicated *family deal* site. I wanted Bubbler to be seen as a customer service focused deal site for families so I needed to ensure that all my business systems and procedures supported great customer service. Therefore, we established a Customer Relationship Management (CRM) system which would allow customers to contact us with any issues and we had a customer service policy where staff needed to respond within 24 hours to enquiries. We encouraged customers to rate their Bubbler experience on our Facebook page so other mums could see it. We backed ourselves and won an award for Best Customer Service, voted by mums in our community. The award acted as a third party endorsement and increased trust in our brand.

We also wanted to position our business as trustworthy and credible so, rather than relying on the exclusive use of PayPal as many small businesses do, we got a bank on board and had an integrated payment system supported by an award-winning third-party gateway. We also listed our Secure Sockets Layer (SSL) certificate details. An SSL allows encrypted data to travel between the web server and another browser providing secure connection between the two. We looked for a partnership that would associate our new business with an established reputable organisation that was highly trusted by our Ideal Mum.

POSITION YOUR BRAND: Busy mums need to be able to find family-friendly deals quickly and they need to trust that the provider is reputable. If they feel valued as a customer, they will be more likely to buy. Bubbler ticked all the boxes for busy mums.

The role of awards

Once you've determined the key differences that make your business special you need to look at how to amplify these differences to your Ideal Mum. Awards are an excellent way to achieve this. They act as a third party endorsement that your business is valued and recognised. If you have an emerging business or one that has recently repositioned itself in the marketplace, I believe that entering awards will support your brand positioning. At Bubbler, we won an award for Best Customer Service, voted by mums in our community, and an award for Best Social Media and both of these supported aspects of the business we valued highly.

CASE STUDY

Nikki Parkinson is a former journalist turned blogger. She has built an award-winning beauty and lifestyle blog called Styling You where she aims to help Australian women over 30 feel confident through their personal style. Styling You has a monthly readership of more than 100,000 and attracts sponsorship from many large national brands. In 2015, Nikki won the Telstra Business Awards Queensland Micro Business of the Year. Being the first blogger to be awarded a Telstra Business Award, Nikki feels the award has provided her with much stronger credibility when negotiating with brands and has brought attention to influencer marketing as a viable marketing strategy to grow sales.

HIGHLIGHT YOUR ACHIEVEMENTS: Winning an award can increase your credibility, visibility and following. You have to enter to win, so look at what is available in your industry sector.

> **ACTION**
> I highly recommend that you seek out and enter
> awards that support your market positioning and how
> you want your brand to be perceived by your Ideal
> Mum. Look at websites such as awardshub.com for
> a list of small business award providers and find what
> might be relevant to you. Seek awards from programs
> your Ideal Mum knows and trusts.

STEP 4: DELIVER AN AWESOME CUSTOMER EXPERIENCE

The one thing we all know about mums is that they are time poor. As a result of this, I've observed they expect a higher degree of customer service than the average consumer. So an excellent opportunity exists for you to differentiate your business by delighting your Ideal Mum, before, during and after her purchase. Simply focus on delivering a superior customer experience. Exceed her expectations and she will notice.

Here are my five tips for delivering an awesome customer experience.

83% of retailers say customer experience is very important to business strategy. Yet, only 30% rate their customer experience > 9/10.

CommBank Retail Insights Report 2016

Tip 1: Be engaged

Mums want to interact with your business – some more than others. If you haven't already got one, create a Facebook business page and start posting some relevant content. A Facebook business page allows your customers to speak with you about things that are relevant to them and this

Truly understand what my problems are and then speak about how your product will solve my problems.

#inmumswords

provides invaluable feedback. It's a great opportunity for you to learn more about your customer base so that you can tailor your service or product more appropriately.

Tip 2: Be responsive

In any business problems arise. It's important that you respond, and quickly. I started my working career as a sales rep selling pet food for Mars Petcare to supermarkets around Victoria. This taught me the importance of the customer. Whenever there was a customer complaint reported to head office, the rep in the area was to drop everything and attend. It was made the number one priority and the company had a clear policy that all customer complaints had to be addressed within 24 hours. It is something that has stayed with me.

You must be timely in your response to a customer's complaint. Mums want to see action. Many an issue has been avoided just by making contact as soon as the complaint is received, acknowledging their concerns and telling them that you will investigate it. Mums want their issues heard quickly – they don't have time to hang around waiting for you. They are juggling enough in their day and want to resolve things so they can move onto their next task. The principle of responding quickly should extend beyond complaints – you really need to be responsive to all contact made by a customer or prospective customer.

I would also stress the importance of delivering what you say you are going to do. Your efforts to be responsive are quickly diminished if you fail to deliver. Make your commitments achievable and ensure you deliver them, and when you can't, get in touch and tell her why.

Tip 3: Be relevant

Do you know what your mum actually wants? To me, part of any good customer service plan is about delivering what the customer wants. I know that as a mum of three young kids, I found the deals hitting my inbox from the mainstream deal sites didn't apply to me. How much IPL and paintballing could one woman want? I started Bubbler largely because the existing offerings in the marketplace lacked any relevance to me. I set up a niche offer which was tailored to mums aged 25–44 years with children aged 12 and under, and delivered against it. I ensured I was relevant to my target market. Straying from this model would see my customer interest drop sharply.

Tip 4: Be extraordinary

Do something unexpected. Go the extra mile every time. It will pay back in droves. Give extraordinary service and people will come to you. They will hear about you from your loyal fans. They will become your best form of advertising. I once had an offer on my site and received some really negative feedback from our members that the venue was unsuitable. Seven complaints came in within 24 hours and I knew I had made an error of judgement in listing this particular business. I looked at the situation from the perspective of a mum and quickly saw that the customers were right. I took the extraordinary step of terminating the agreement with the merchant and writing to every person who had made a purchase, apologising and informing them that we didn't feel the deal was suitable. All customers were refunded within three working days. This speedy response was unexpected by my customers. We received a huge volume of positive feedback. We built trust. Our customers felt very confident purchasing on our site as they knew that if something went wrong our business would address it. These customers continued to purchase from our site and refer other friends. See page 21 for more detail.

Tip 5: Be respectful

I think it's incredibly important to put yourself in the shoes of your customers. Be respectful of their time and how and when you communicate with them. If you target busy mums with young families it makes sense that you don't try and engage with them at dinnertime but rather after the kids have gone to bed. This ensures a better response for your efforts.

At Bubbler, one of the key things I witnessed on other deal sites was 'deal fatigue'. Customers were unsubscribing from sites or had stopped buying because the offers were irrelevant or they were having their inbox bombarded with three emails each day for the one deal. Customers felt spammed. So we issued only one email for each new deal launched. By being respectful of our customer's inbox, we had an email open rate much higher than the industry standard. In fact I've often heard from people that they actually enjoy opening their Bubbler email and seeing what our latest deal is.

Be real about what it is like to be a mum. It's not glamorous all the time so don't try to make it feel like it is. It is challenging but rewarding. It's filled with bad hair days full of love, exhaustion and memories made on a daily basis.

#inmumswords

There are some things you can specifically implement into your business to deliver an awesome customer experience. These include strategies for online and bricks-and-mortar stores as well as money-back guarantees, free trials and personalising the experience.

Online strategies

If you are an online business, ensure that your website is mobile friendly and is fast to download, given mums have a short attention span thanks to all the interruptions in their day. Google reports that people are five times more likely to abandon a website which is not mobile friendly. Download speed is also critically important – half of all mobile visitors will leave your website if it takes more than three (yes, three) seconds to download.

Thankfully Google has released a great tool to test both mobile friendliness and download speed. I have tested my own website, getting 100 per cent for mobile friendliness but testing poor for speed, which I was unaware of and quickly changed. To make things really easy, they also provide a report on what you need to do specifically to solve this, all delivered within 60 seconds.

Be mindful that mums demand minimal clicks to make their purchases with easy payment options. PayPal often suits a busy mum on her phone as she only needs to remember her PayPal password rather than pulling out her credit card. Consider a scrolling website that allows you to take your prospective customer through a well-researched and thought-out path to purchase. This should include the problems your Ideal Mum faces and how you solve them, followed by testimonials for third party endorsement and a strong call to action. It literally becomes your sales funnel and it is likely to reduce bounce rates and increase your sales conversions.

Be aware that most purchases involve mums looking at multiple platforms (website, social media and third party websites) and across multiple devices (smartphone and desktop) before the purchase is made.

Mums also need to quickly understand what your business does and why your product or service is beneficial to them; clearly communicated in an engaging headline and easily viewed when they land on your website. Think about adding a chat line to your website and displaying a security seal on your payment page.

You need to delight her at every stage along her path to purchase. Look at how you welcome your mum when she signs up to receive your newsletter. Do you have an email sequence that she receives, so you can learn more

Cut out the crap! Ditch the sales jargon and cut to the chase. Mums aren't stupid but we are time poor and tired with a very low tolerance for 'BS'. Tell us what you sell, why we need it, make it honest good value with no catch and we'll buy it, done deal!

#inmumswords

about her and allow her to segment her preferences? This is important in developing a relationship with your Ideal Mum and preventing her from unsubscribing.

Look at your shipping costs. Many mums are starting to expect free shipping offers especially if they spend a lot of money. Look to avoid excessive shipping costs as mums will abandon their shopping carts in droves. 'Click & Collect' is often a great way to attract mums who want the convenience of placing the order online and picking it up when it suits them.

Bricks-and-mortar stores

Mums are frequently time poor and they also want to feel valued. Always look to go the extra mile for your Ideal Mum – be engaged, responsive and attentive to helping her solve her problems.

There are organisations that offer great real time data and will track traffic within your store. It will identify customer hotspots and their particular preferences. Armed with this knowledge you can place your higher margin products in the most attractive place.

Is your store merchandised in a way that encourages your Ideal Mum to meander through? For example, if you are targeting mums with young children, can they wheel their pusher through your store layout? Do you have a play area for kids or a ramp to assist your Ideal Mum to get her pusher in the door?

We are seeing bricks-and-mortar stores going online and online stores opening pop-up stores so the distinction between the two is blurring and it is becoming harder for a business to gain the attention of mums. For example, Kogan started as an online business and now has a pop-up bricks-and-mortar store. If you deliver an incredible customer experience at all stages along the path to purchase and after sales contact, you're more likely to get mum's attention, and retain her as a customer. If you offer delivery, give her good options – maybe offer Click & Collect so she doesn't have to pay for shipping and can pop in when it suits her or send someone on her behalf.

Money-back guarantees and free trials

Another strategy to improve your customer's experience is a well communicated and promoted money-back guarantee or free trial. This can reduce barriers to purchase and allow your Ideal Mum to try you out. This applies to both instore and online experiences. Shopify, a business offering a complete ecommerce solution, quoted a study that saw a 21 per cent sales increase with the addition of a money-back guarantee. For this to be successful you need to clearly state the conditions under which the money-back guarantee or free trial will operate so there are no nasty surprises for your Ideal Mum. You need to make sure the strategy actually works for you.

Do some research into whether a money-back guarantee or a free trial would work best for you. If in doubt, go and ask your community. It might be as simple as posting the question on your business's Facebook page or asking the advice of other small business owners operating in similar industries to see what their experience has been.

Do not be pushy. Get me the facts and price and I'll work out whether it's right for me.

#inmumswords

Feedback from the Marketing to Mums survey shows that mums don't want to part with their money without an opportunity to trial the product first. They want to reduce the perceived risk of engaging your service or purchasing your product so a money-back guarantee or free trial might allow you to overcome this obstacle and make mums' experience with your business more trustworthy and enjoyable.

Personalisation

Mums love to be made to feel special, so don't treat them like they are all the same. Can you personalise your messages to them? Bronto, a commerce marketing automation provider, reports that 'segmentation increases click-throughs and drives lift rates as much as six times higher than sending a message to the entire list'. Segmentation allows you to send more tailored sales messages and promotions of your database. Yes, it requires

68% of shoppers are more likely to return to a store that remembers them. 74% also agree they will stay loyal to a business that personalises their experience.

CommBank Retail Insights Report 2016

some work to set up but strong segmentation will assist you to deliver a better customer experience and, in turn, increase sales conversions.

Can you personalise an offer based on the cart abandonment history of the buyer? If you had a customer who had a number of woollen jumpers they abandoned in their cart on the previous visit to your online store, can you offer them 10 per cent off next time they visit? And if they are not a signed subscriber, could you make this offer in exchange for their email? Do you hold a customer's sales history when they visit your bricks-and-mortar store? This would allow your sales staff to make better product suggestions and increase sales conversions.

✔ CHECKLIST

Things to do to improve your customer experince:

❍ Employ more women – CommBank research shows those businesses who rated their customer experience as 9/10 or more had a significantly higher number of female employees in leadership roles.

❍ Keep your customer avatar above everyone's desk. Everything they do in their day should be keeping her top of mind.

○ Improve your website, ensuring minimal clicks, easily found FAQs, a chat system to answer queries online immediately to improve conversions, set the limits on amount of time permitted before a customer query is answered.

○ Put yourself in your Ideal Mum's shoes when dealing with any negative feedback.

○ Establish a process for dealing with customer queries, complaints and praise.

○ Ask your customers if there are products or services they would like to see added to your offerings.

○ Introduce a loyalty program.

○ Have a follow-up system post sale to understand mums' feedback about your product or service.

○ Ensure your staff are well trained about your Ideal Mum and her challenges so they can serve her better.

○ Can you personalise the experience for her in any way? Can you track her sales history and offer her similar new items when they're available?

○ Can you value-add to your offer by providing bonus products or free WiFi for her use?

○ How can you remember each customer's name when they walk in? Can you track their previous purchases?

○ How can you make mum feel special and valued? For example, a VIP shopping night for your best clients to preview all new season gear, with a special offer.

○ Invite her to join your newsletter and social media so you can stay engaged with her post purchase.

When I worked in the corporate world, I frequented a small fashion boutique in Richmond. It was by no means cheap, in fact the clothes were priced outside my budget but the owner was an absolute professional at nurturing and developing a great customer relationship. I always enjoyed an incredible experience in her store and always walked out buying a lot more than I intended to. Why? She had a knack for knowing exactly what would and wouldn't work for my body shape which saved me plenty of time and frustration going through the racks myself. She personalised my experience by always noting down what I liked but didn't buy. She would call to tell me when she had reduced particular items I'd liked on previous visits or clothing that would match the outfit I had already purchased, and would put them aside for me. I marvelled at her ability as a salesperson – she could get me to spend much more than I had intended and left me feeling really good. This business wowed me with an incredible customer experience. They reduced all the barriers to purchase and made it very easy for me to buy. She would upsell on a later date with complementary products. She showed a genuine interest in helping me.

AWESOME CUSTOMER EXPERIENCE: By personalising the shopping experience, a small boutique saved busy women time and reduced their frustration when shopping for clothes, which in turn generated increased sales and repeat business.

ACTION

Use the Google tool to test your speed and confirm if you are mobile friendly by going to <https://testmysite. thinkwithgoogle.com/> and inserting your domain name. If you are not mobile friendly, you need to work with a web developer to fix this promptly, particularly given that mum is doing the bulk of her interactions from her smartphone. Make it a priority.

Review your existing customer experience both before, during and after purchase. List at least ten ways you can delight your customers and implement at least five of these, ensuring they are communicated to all people in your organisation.

STEP 5: FIND YOUR PARTNERS

A great marketing partnership has mutually beneficial outcomes for two or more businesses. The partnerships might include a joint competition, a referral or affiliate program or valuable add-on benefits to your clients.

Forming partnerships is, without question, one of simplest and most cost-effective methods of increasing your sales yet I'd say that only a relatively small proportion of businesses are actively utilising partnerships to grow their business. I am very committed to marketing partnerships in my businesses; they have given me solid growth without the need for a large marketing budget. What's not to like? They have also provided me with the great satisfaction of growing my business alongside others, while knowing that there are equally beneficial outcomes for all partners.

I was approached by a major airline magazine to see if I was interested in investing $12,000 for an advertisement in their magazine. When I explained that I could get that same reach through a marketing partnership which might cost me $50 and deliver considerably more email sign-ups than the case study they referenced, they were floored and had no comeback but to congratulate me on my work. So now I want to show you how you can deliver yourself $12,000 in advertising value for well under $100. Have I got your attention?

Firstly you need to have a really good understanding of what you want to achieve and what things a potential partner might value that you can offer.

You might have won awards, so potential partners might want to be associated with your success. A larger business might be attracted by your smaller size because you can be nimble and responsive to market pressures. One of the key things I was able to offer larger businesses was that I could negotiate and administer a partnership between a group of three or more businesses. This was highly attractive as the larger business invested minimal time but still got to enjoy the positive outcomes. The trick here is to think broadly about your skills or those of your business that might be valued by another complementary business.

CHECKLIST

Look at this list as a starting point in assessing what you can offer:

- ❍ Number of members or clients
- ❍ Number of fans on your Facebook or Instagram
- ❍ Content such as blog articles or how-to videos
- ❍ Your contacts/suppliers
- ❍ Awards you have won
- ❍ Case studies/insights you can share
- ❍ Specific skills you might have
- ❍ Your attitude and approach to business

CASE STUDY

I have previously teamed up with a female-led IT business to pitch a story to Fairfax Media. We were successful in our pitch, providing the journalist with a story around mums getting into online businesses. The story featured in *The Age* and Fairfax online raising our respective profiles nationally and attracting interest amongst the investing community. Marketing partnerships can be used to grow your email database, find new leads, add value to existing clients to gain their loyalty or to position your business.

PARTNER FOR MUTUAL BENEFIT: Monetary outcomes might not be the only result you're after when it comes to partnering up to promote your business.

CHOODIE is an innovative beach gown company, invented by a Perth mum who wanted to minimise the need for lugging towels to the pool or beach. I had featured them on a Bubbler deal campaign and such was their popularity it temporarily crashed the Bubbler website.

I was undertaking a major survey of our database to gain some further business insights. Firstly, this would enable me to have some statistics around our database to assist potential advertisers and secondly, I'd be able to gain greater insights about our audience to enable us to secure other potential partners. To make the survey credible, it was really important to get a solid response rate, so I wanted to give away a prize to survey respondents. I knew my Ideal Mum's time was very limited so the reward of a competition prize encouraged her to take two minutes out of her day to complete it. This was also a great marketing partnership opportunity.

I approached Choodie because I knew that my community loved this product and it would gain my Ideal Mum's attention. I set up a marketing partnership where Choodie provided ten of their products to be won by people who completed the survey and answered a competition question. In return, we provided Choodie with ongoing advertising to our then community of 100,000 for the four-week duration. Both parties benefitted. We ended up with great data and Choodie enjoyed four weeks of exposure to their ideal target market. This data has provided greater detail for our potential advertisers but, perhaps more importantly, enabled us to identify other potential partnerships we wanted to pursue. For example, we were able to establish the percentage splits of where Bubbler mums do their grocery shopping each week, allowing us to present an opportunity for one of the supermarket retailers to work with us and to provide a sales story around why mums should change from the competing supermarket retailer.

PARTNER FOR MUTUAL BENEFIT: There were mutual benefits for Bubbler and Choodie when the beach gown company provided competition prizes for the Bubbler mums who completed a market research data survey. Great data for Bubbler, great exposure for Choodie.

CASE STUDY

FAMILY FOOD WORKS is run by Eve Reed, a paediatric dietitian from New South Wales. She wanted to tap into our network by providing some relevant content to our community about how to deal with toddlers' eating issues. She approached us and was able to articulate that there was 'a need for reliable, professional information about children's nutrition'. We knew that this would be of great interest to our community as we had received huge sales from a toddler seat that reduced mealtime stress. Eve wrote a blog article called 'Top 5 Tips for Fussy Eaters' and she shared some strategies with our mums. The blog received over 850 clicks, she enjoyed over 50 downloads of her eBook that provided further information about her business and new people signed up to her newsletter.

PARTNER FOR MUTUAL BENEFIT: Family Food Works gave Bubbler content that was relevant to the community of mums, therefore keeping them engaged; in turn, Eve Reed was able to extend the reach of her services.

> **ACTION**
> Before you can really get into forming partnerships,
> you need to be clear about your business goals and
> what you want to achieve. These objectives need to
> be specific and measurable. I recommend you spend
> some time listing your business's key objectives. Now
> write down all the skills and access you could offer a
> potential partner.

Identifying potential partners

Once you have a list of what you can offer, you can start
to identify potential partners. The first thing I look for
when brainstorming partnerships are businesses who have
the same target market as my business but who are not
in direct competition with me. This means they operate
within my industry and have relevance to my Ideal Mum
but she could be interested in both my business's offering
and a potential partner's.

You will be surprised at how many come to mind.
Most of the best potential partners will be businesses you
know and interact with already. This is where you can
achieve a lot of quick wins and it's certainly where I would
recommend you start.

For example, given that Bubbler is an award-winning
shopping website which targets mums aged 25–44 years
and who have children under 12 years old, I looked for

parenting websites that targeted mums in the same age range with primary school-aged children. I would research prospective partners by looking at their website's About Us section and reading their Facebook page. This generally would give me a good feel for the business. Next, I'd check out what people were saying about that potential partner. I would google reviews for the business also. You want to ensure that the potential partner's brand attributes are in keeping with yours and do not violate your brand value.

This is a great opportunity to think laterally. You should be aiming to identify businesses that hold similar brand values to your business and share a target market, but your product or service offering could be quite different.

> **ACTION**
> Make a list of all potential partners you know that match your target audience. Then make a second list where you consider businesses you don't know or businesses that operate in other industries that you believe are targeting the same Ideal Mum as you.

Making contact

Now that you have got a clear understanding of what you bring to a partnership and a list of potential partners, start thinking about making contact. If a company is unknown to me, I will tend to do a bit of research first. I'll call the head office and find out who I would need to speak to (and often ask for their email and direct phone number at this time also). I will then google them to find out a bit more and to gauge whether they might be open to a partnership. Typically this involves looking at their LinkedIn profile. If you don't want them to see that you are viewing them, change your settings to anonymous first. Look for common interests or insights into their personality.

Then take the plunge – reach out and cold call. I have made my best marketing partnerships and strategic alliances from approaches on LinkedIn, Facebook or through picking up the phone. Most other business owners respect people who make the effort to make the approach. A word of caution though: be respectful of their time and ensure you are offering to bring something that is genuinely mutually beneficial otherwise you can damage your credibility.

Brainstorming ideas

A short chat to discuss mutually beneficial business outcomes is a good start. I find entering a brainstorming discussion to be particularly insightful. Not only can it introduce an idea that you hadn't thought of, it allows you to understand how your potential partner thinks, what they value and you can find out more about their Ideal Mum.

Be more relatable so we feel you understand our world. Portray 'real' life rather than the fluffy pretty ads of mostly not-real life that just make us feel worse! Make us laugh. Engage us. It will make our sleep-deprived brains remember you.

#inmumswords

Look at creating promotional partnerships around special events such as Mother's Day or get really creative and look at a 'School's back, Mum relax!' style of promotion where you could partner up with a number of suitable businesses to celebrate mums sending the kids back to school and now having some time to themselves.

Formalise your partnership

Once you've had a verbal discussion and confirmed how you see the partnership working, it's time to formalise your marketing partnership by putting it in writing. I find a simple two- to three-page document works best. In my marketing partnership documents

I provide a summary of the joint marketing project, then list all the businesses involved and the assets they possess before listing what each party will do in the partnership. I go into a fair bit of detail about each business's obligations as this is where I've seen other marketing partnerships come unstuck. I always ask each party to sign it as their commitment to fulfilling their obligations and I monitor each commitment. One great way to manage a limited-time marketing partnership with more than two businesses is to set up a group Facebook page where you can share information. This might be the place you post to show that you are fulfilling each of your promotional obligations in the partnership.

ACTION

Make a commitment to your business to meet with, say, one to three suitable businesses over the next 60 days. Your objective is to secure a minimum of one marketing partnership which you can implement and then measure the outcomes of within the next 90 days. Make sure you have measurements against the objective you are wanting to achieve. This could include growth of community, number of new client leads, email sign-ups or sales.

STEP 6: BUILD YOUR LIST

One of the key responsibilities you have in your business is to develop your assets so that should you decide to exit your business, you have something to sell. Your database or customer list is one of these assets.

A database list is a collection of the email addresses of people who match your Ideal Mum target market. It should be a combination of existing customers and prospects. Your email list might be separated by different characteristics such as location, whether they are a customer or prospect or other such factors. You might record their full name and email or just their email address.

Stop promoting picture perfect and promote normal. Reassure us it's OK to have bad days and carry baby weight. Give us real opinions from real mums.

#inmumswords

You might segment your list to reflect a mum's preferences. Businesses use their database to regularly communicate with their Ideal Mum and to develop relationships and to increase their sales. Email marketing will deliver the greatest conversions of sales, outperforming social media. Unlike Facebook, it is something that you own and you can control the communications with your Ideal Mum. It allows you to build a deeper relationship and it's an effective selling tool. That's why your focus should always be on growing your list.

There are many suppliers available to assist you to manage and communicate with your list. For many small businesses with small lists there are free or very low-cost packages available, including MailChimp which has a free service for under 2000 sign-ups. For those with a vision to grow a large list or wanting to establish a sales funnel where you send out a communication sequence to your customers or prospects, you should look at programs such as Infusionsoft and AWeber.

To grow your email database of Ideal Mums, there are four great strategies you can use:

→ Sales funnel
→ Referral program
→ Marketing partnerships
→ Website tools including pop-ups, sliders and floating footers

Sales funnel

Remember women take more time to make their purchase decision. They need lots of interactions with your brand along the way. You need to funnel your Ideal Mum along in a journey from meeting you to making a transaction, and then encourage her to stay around for re-purchasing your service or product.

One way you can do this is to set up a sales funnel, which is a sequence of communications and events you want to guide your Ideal Mum through before a sale takes place. Consider what relevant information or tips that relate to your product or her life you could give away for free as a getting-to-know-you gift in exchange for her email address. This might include an infographic, checklist, eBook, how-to blog article or a mistakes-to-avoid list.

Facebook advertising is another method you can use to funnel prospective mums onto your email list. Jon Loomer, a respected digital marketing consultant in the US, believes in a four-step process of growing your list:

→ Attracting relevant fans
→ Providing them some value (free relevant and valued content as previously identified)
→ Gaining their email address
→ Selling

What I like about Jon's approach is that it allows plenty of time for you to share your brand story, show your value and really earn your Ideal Mum's trust before a sale takes place. I believe it is these kind of connections with your Ideal Mum that will be the most lasting. Your job is to identify the journey you want to take your Ideal Mum on, from her first point of contact with you through to a transaction with your business.

Referral program

Imagine your Ideal Mum acting as your brand ambassador and bringing her friends along to purchase your product or service. A systemised referral program can do this for you. It will facilitate word-of-mouth marketing and enable the mum-to-mum recommendations that we understand are so important.

Don't rely on computer cookies and my search history to advertise as it just makes your advertising seem dull and repetitive.

#inmumswords

   A referral program will only work if your mum has a great experience in working with or purchasing from you. This means it's crucial that you wow your mum with not just a good but an *awesome* customer experience. Before you can start devising an awesome referral program to build your list, you need to ensure your customers are enjoying a great experience. You cannot rely on the referrals to just come in automatically – you need to have a strategy that you implement. You need to show your Ideal Mum how she can refer you to her friends. Effectively, you need to show your happy customer how to act as an ambassador for your product or service. In doing so, she is likely to become even more loyal to your business. In devising your referral program make sure your reward is valued by your Ideal Mum and doesn't cost you too much. You also need to ensure it is not too complicated to action or she just won't do it.

At Bubbler we highlighted our referral program that enabled mums who were already members to earn $5 in Bubbler credit by referring their friends, if they made a purchase within 14 days. Essentially we were rewarding existing customers for recommending us to their friends. Because they were rewarded with credit to use next time they made a purchase, we were also ensuring future sales. This assisted us to add thousands of new mums to our database.

One idea you might wish to consider is to identify your best customers and provide them with a special incentive if they refer their friends. For example, you might be holding an exclusive special shopping night to launch your new collection with champagne and canapes. You could provide your Ideal Mum with five tickets so she can bring her friends along. This is a special night to reward your VIPs who can enjoy the first look at the new collection, but equally you understand your mum doesn't get much time to go out with her girlfriends and enjoy a glass of champagne so you suggest she brings them along too. If you are an online store you could provide your best customers with a special code for their friends to use in the next two weeks to receive 15 per cent off all your new season products.

If you are a service-based business, you can set up an affiliate program providing them with 5–10 per cent of the new client's bookings or consider simply thanking them for their referral by delivering a gift box with something valued by the recipient. This can encourage them to continue the behaviour. I recently watched a video on social media where the hosts of the #BusinessAddicts podcast received a gift from a business which they mentioned on their podcast. The excitement and joy expressed by the hosts as they opened their gift was infectious and the reach and brand awareness received by the gift givers was *huge* so be generous and show gratitude towards your referrers.

Your referral program doesn't necessarily need to cost you anything. You might implement a content referral strategy where you post engaging content on your Facebook page which can be shared by your Ideal Mum. At Bubbler we grew our Facebook page enormously by implementing this strategy. For example, we posted a question to our community about what was the worst thing someone said to you when pregnant. The post received over 150 comments and reached over 40,000 people. Many fans tagged their friends (other mums) and brought them into the conversation resulting in an increase in the number of Ideal Mums joining our Facebook community and starting a relationship with our business. This is not something we do here and there; we have a formalised schedule that identifies our posts and is designed to engage and attract new Ideal Mums to our community.

Another idea might be to ask for referrals when you are speaking to your happy customers or put a statement at the end of your purchase page asking people to forward this on to three friends.

Marketing partnerships

We've talked about the enormous value of strategic marketing partnerships, and it's worth noting they can be a very effective and low-cost way to build your list. A great partnership will expose your business to thousands of your Ideal Mums. Think about things like running a competition with a partner and making it a condition that entrants sign up to your mailing list. Do this in conjunction with a select few businesses who also share your Ideal Mum target market. For more on marketing partnerships, see pages 117 to 127.

Website list building: sliders, pop-ups and floating footer bars

It is amazing how a few tweaks on your website can dramatically increase your email list. I recently read a study from Kevan Lee, content crafter at Buffer, a platform allowing you to save time and drive engagement on social media, who was able to build their email list by 130 per cent on the previous month by increasing their email capture methods from one to nine.

Have real mums review your products and advertise them. Not celebrities or supermodel mums – just normal mums who don't always have it together and are struggling with life just like I am!

#inmumswords

Pop-ups are considered to be very annoying. They literally pop up after a certain amount of seconds and many businesses do not allow you to close them but force you to enter your email address before proceeding any further to their website. While they get the highest number of email sign-ups they don't appear to value the relationship with the prospective customer. A pop-up can be seen as an obstacle, resulting in a drop in page visits and time spend on your website so proceed with caution. You can reduce the obstacle of a pop-up by having it appear after a certain time on your website. Additionally, you can look to ensure it is not so large that it prevents your Ideal Mum from accessing the key information they are trying to get from your website. Finally, make sure the viewer can choose to close your pop-up. I really believe that pop-ups that don't allow you to proceed to a website are far more likely to irritate your Ideal Mum, thereby starting your relationship on the wrong foot. Look for a well-positioned one which appears after a delay and can be closed. For all the bad press pop-ups might get, you can program them to appear as a one-off which is what I would tend to favour.

A less intrusive option and one favoured by many bloggers are sliders. These might either slide up or slide across your website and invite someone to sign up to your mailing list or download a free gift. The very nature of them sliding in gets the viewer's attention and most sliders are relatively small so do not always stop a viewer's ability to read the website. I've researched this extensively, and it appears that people are getting the best results by having their slider appear anywhere from 60–80 per cent of the way down the page. The added advantage of using a slider is that you have the ability to add a cookie to ensure that it doesn't appear again for a certain period of time. This is particularly important in the case of mums. They are already being bombarded with sales messages and actionable tasks so if you choose to add a slider, which I believe you should, ensure you factor in a non-display period also.

Another tool you could consider are sticky bars.

These can be located either at the top or bottom of your page inviting a visitor to sign up to your mailing list. As the viewer scrolls down the page the sticky bar remains visible. They are also referred to as 'hello bars' or 'floating footer bars'. The bar can be closed by the viewer and you have the ability to program it so that it doesn't reappear for a certain number of days.

Sign-up boxes are perhaps the most common form of email capture, however multiple studies have shown that they don't work as effectively as the slider or pop-up. I think this is largely a design issue. We kind of skim over certain parts of websites to home in on our regular section. There exists a bit of website blindness. I think this only encourages businesses to either look at redesigning their sites on a regular basis or employ more email list building methods.

Most people decide on whether or not to subscribe to your website and/or blog after reading your content so it would make sense to invite them to subscribe at the end of your content delivery. Consider adding an inbuilt sign-up section at the bottom of your About Us section and under each of your blogs. Make sure the language that you use appeals to your Ideal Mum.

At Bubbler we utilised a combination of a pop-up, slider and sign-up box. We used a variety with some coding to ensure we were not irritating our Ideal Mum. We used a pop-up that appeared as a one-off when a new device accessed our website. We did this to minimise any annoyance this might create for our mum. We also used a slider on our blog, via a free WordPress plug-in called SumoMe. We programmed it so that it slid up when people approached the bottom third of our blog so as not to irritate them. There is also a sharing option so that mums can share blog content they deem worthy with friends via social media.

Your website landing page and About Us pages are the ideal place to feature a sign-up box. These are often the most visited pages on a website. You can check via Google Analytics to see which pages customers like to visit to identify where you should feature the box.

So I encourage you to look at how you could increase the opportunities for capturing emails whether instore or online. Don't rely on just one. The greater the number of opportunities, the faster your list will grow. There are lots of great applications out there that will now allow you to program when and how often communication appears to ensure you are not irritating your mum. Use them and you will grow your list of happy mums.

ACTION
Establish the best email list building activities for your business and implement them into your business in the next 90 days.

STEP 7: GET SOCIAL

Mums are spending an increasing amount of time on social media. According to the 2016 Sensis Social Media Report, Australians are spending 24 minutes each time they check Facebook, a significant jump from the previous four Social Media reports which recorded 17–18 minutes per visit. I suspect this is being driven by mums and their incredible appetite for social media. In 2012, a Facebook Nielsen study reported that 78 per cent of Australian mums were checking Facebook every day.

Armed with her trusty smartphone, mum is checking her social media throughout the day whenever she has a few minutes and then she enjoys a longer, less interrupted session once the kids are in bed. The Sensis Social Media Report also states that more than 40 per cent of Australian women who are social media users are accessing their social media while watching TV. It highlights the diminishing impact of TV advertising as mums are generally distracted by their social media updates.

If mums are enjoying so much time on social media, shouldn't your business be there too?

One of the key attractions of social media is that it allows for two-way communication, in sharp contrast to traditional media. It is one of the most cost-effective marketing mediums available and it can deliver incredible insights for your business. Generally, social media can help you develop deeper relationships with your customers.

CHECKLIST

Think about these reasons for being active on social media:

- ○ Sharing your brand story
- ○ Developing trust and rapport leading to increased loyalty
- ○ Generating leads and growing your email list
- ○ Facilitating mum-to-mum recommendations
- ○ Increasing brand awareness
- ○ Driving traffic to your website or store to make sales
- ○ Gaining insights about your Ideal Mum
- ○ Demonstrating your superior customer service
- ○ Gaining feedback about new products, promotions, packaging and more

I passionately believe that social media marketing is essential for any business that primarilytargets mums. A Social Media Examiner report in 2015 found that 'spending as little as 6 hours per week, 66 per cent of marketers see lead generation benefits with social media' and '81 per cent of participants found that increased traffic occurred with as little as 6 hours per week invested in social media marketing'. Similarly, the Sensis Social Media Report states that small and medium-sized businesses that invest in social media experience increased sales and profitability compared to those who do not use social media.

Despite the incredible advantages social media provides businesses and marketers, the Sensis report finds that only 48 per cent of small businesses and 54 per cent of medium businesses have a social media presence. Large businesses have grasped the social media opportunity with almost 80 per cent engaging in social media. While this statistic is significantly higher, I am still surprised and perplexed when I see large businesses not harnessing the power of social media given their resource availability. Last year I spoke with a large brand which is a household name, targets Australian mums and is sold in all our major supermarkets. Not only did they not have a social media strategy but they had not secured their brand's social media name assets.

When engaging in any new activity, it is essential you have a plan. Only 31 per cent of small businesses and 36 per cent of medium businesses have a strategic plan for social media. Your social media strategy document should identify which social media platforms your Ideal Mum uses and then you can tailor your efforts according.

Your social media strategy should include how you will drive awareness, traffic and increase your following to your nominated social media accounts. It should also include how often you will post and how much of your posting will be engaging content and how much will be sales content. I strongly advocate doing one platform well before moving on to another.

CHECKLIST

There are a number of ways you can drive traffic to your social media accounts:

○ Ensure your social media icons are prominently featured on your website. I featured mine twice on each webpage. They appeared in the top right hand corner where members signed in to their Bubbler account and then again at the website footer.

○ Include links to sign up to social media platforms when you send out your confirmation email.

○ Feature your social media icons on your newsletter communications every time.

○ Feature social media icons on all your marketing materials including brochures and in any traditional media you engage in.

○ Follow other businesses with the same target audience as you. Note: do not spam other pages with posts such as 'Hello from your newest liker @BubblerDeals' as this is deemed unprofessional and will have you banned from the page.

○ Schedule posts consistently at peak times when your Ideal Mum is online (first thing in the morning and again in the evening). Consistency will benefit your reach.

○ See what your community is responding to in your newsletter and promote this on your social media channels to drive traffic to your website.

○ Cross-promote amongst your social media platforms.

○ Ensure you use conversational language, include strong calls to action in your sales posts and avoid using words like 'win', 'competition' or 'giveaway' in promoting any online competitions.

○ Find your social media influencers and look to run a joint competition or create a joint product or project together.

○ Create a dialogue with your community to strengthen relationships. Encourage your community to share how they use your product. This provides you with third party proof and validates your product/service for others.

There are lots of social media platforms, but I am going to focus on the two most popular among Australian mums: Facebook and Instagram. This is where businesses are enjoying the best sales conversions in targeting Australian mums and I believe you should focus on getting these two right before considering other platforms.

Facebook

Australians are considered some of the heaviest users of Facebook in the world according to a report by Nielsen in 2015. There are 10 million Australians active on Facebook every day. Given 9 million of these are accessing Facebook via a mobile you can be sure mums make up a healthy

> Publish independent reviews of products so we can weigh up all the information.
>
> **#inmumswords**

proportion of them. In the Marketing to Mums Survey Australian mums rated Facebook as their number one social media platform. More than a quarter of mums stated they check in to their Facebook account more than ten times every day. Facebook is more popular with older mums while younger mums seem to favour Instagram.

I have found Facebook far outperforms Instagram in driving sales. Despite the algorithm changes you might have heard of, this is still the best social media platform to invest in for businesses who target mums. Facebook allows you to build deeper relationships, drive traffic and gain greater insights into your Ideal Mum. This can then allow you to better target her in other ways such as developing a new product or service which will better solve her problems. This may give you a significant advantage over competitors and drive sales growth.

ACTION

If you haven't already secured all your brand and business names for Facebook, Instagram, Twitter, LinkedIn, Snapchat and YouTube please do it before someone else does. It is worth securing all social media addresses even if you decide to focus on just one or two as things might change in the future.

I want to share with you my top nine tips to consider when using Facebook for business.

Tip 1 – Engaging content is key for mums

Entertain mum! She is seeking engaging and useful content. Use a variety of media (video, graphics, article links) and don't skimp on your graphics. Mum has a short attention span so grab her with a great graphic. Capitalise on the trend of Australians watching video content on Facebook and feature video on your page. In fact why not share your brand story via video? Video not only increases reach, it provides you with an opportunity to show why you are passionate about what you do and to tell your Ideal Mum what she means to you. Mums are overwhelmed by the sheer amount of content available to them on social media so your content needs to stand out. Focus on information that is useful – you will only know what is useful if you have carried out solid research into your Ideal Mum in step one.

Mum loves humour too. We have had great success sharing memes and graphics of mums having a laugh at themselves. Organic Valley, an independent cooperative of organic farmers in the US, produced a great video for Facebook which went viral internationally in April 2016. They poked fun at the unrealistic stereotypical depiction of mums on television advertisements which mums found particularly amusing. Organic Valley then told it as it really is. In doing so, they showed they really understand the juggle of getting out the door in the mornings and that some mornings you just need to grab-and-go with breakfast. They used humour very effectively to highlight the problem and present their organic 'breakfast in a bottle' product as the solution. They supported the social media campaign with a dedicated website called RealMorningReport.com where 'moms' could complete an online survey to receive a free trial of their product.

Think about content that will be really useful for your Ideal Mum. This might include free tips, hacks or solutions you can share. BuzzSumo.com is a very useful website for finding engaging content that is trending online to share on your Facebook page. You can search by topic such as 'Mother's Day' or 'Back to School' to find engaging content that relates to your business. This tip will save you huge amounts of time and ensure you are publishing trending content. It's a great discovery if you haven't used it already and it is free to use.

Marketing partnerships with other businesses can be a great way to receive content too. If you have a community that is interested in recipes, is there a food business you could partner with who could supply you with recipes to share amongst your community? At Bubbler we ran two very successful marketing partnerships with food-planning businesses that provided us with a recipe each week to promote on Facebook. Our mums loved that we gave them something new to try as most of them find thinking about what to cook for dinner exhausting. The recipe providers benefitted as they were able to communicate with a community of their Ideal Mums.

Another method of creating content is to introduce a blog to your website. At Bubbler we featured a blog post on behalf of a client, Stuff Masters, showcasing their Launch Pods, a locker system they have developed for the home to organise all the kids' school stuff including school bag, uniform, lunch items and special notes. We provided an authentic endorsement of the product as our social media manager had just purchased and was using the Stuff Masters Launch Pods. The blog post received over 3400 click-throughs of their Ideal Mum. This blog was so popular because the content solved the problem of how to keep all the school stuff in one place so the house remained clean and things didn't get lost. These blogs can then be promoted on your Facebook page to drive traffic to your website.

Tip 2 – Learn about your mum

Facebook is one of the best ways to find out more about your community. If you have an established page, the first thing I would be doing is visiting Page Insights. In particular, look to see what posts your fans are hiding and don't want you to see. This is rarely checked by most businesses but it's very useful in developing your content and learning about what does *not* interest your mum.

I would also encourage you to engage with your community on a daily basis. There is no more effective way to understand them than talking with them online. I recommend spending 15 minutes each evening commenting, liking and responding to things that your fans have posted. On Bubbler I frequently asked them about what deals they'd like to see coming up on our website. This assisted me to identify potential deal campaigns that were more likely to deliver greater sales simply by asking them and learning more about what they wanted. They liked that they were being heard and I appreciated learning more about what kind of deals they wanted me to secure for them. The more accurately I could establish what they wanted, the more sales I was able to make.

The housework is generally shared and this needs to be promoted.

#inmumswords

Tip 3 – Great cover photo

I recommend having an eye-catching cover image on your Facebook page to grab mum's attention. The sizing of your Facebook cover page depends on whether it is being accessed from a desktop (828 pixels wide x 315 pixels high) or mobile phone (640 pixels wide x 360 pixels high). You need to ensure it displays well for both devices, however pay particular attention to the mobile sizing as we know that mums are more likely to access their social media from their smartphone. Facebook recommends sizing at 851 pixels x 315 pixels and less than 100kb will have the fastest load times. Your Facebook cover page should have a strong call to action such as a sign-up to your newsletter or your tagline so a first-time visitor understands exactly what you do and what action you want them to take.

I recommend updating your image regularly, every few months, to keep it fresh and ensure mum actually sees it. You may wish to reflect different sales seasons such as Back to School, Easter, Christmas or EOFY (End of Financial Year). Alternatively, you might change it to reflect a different call to action or you might wish to allow a sponsor to co-brand your Facebook cover image temporarily for a particular event you might be working with them on as part of an integrated advertising package.

Tip 4 – Tell your story

Be authentic and tell your brand story on Facebook. I will periodically do a post about who I am, why I started the business and invite mums to tell me about their families.

If you are a mum-led business you are definitely at an advantage compared to other businesses. Mums love to support other mums. They also love it when mums go into business because they invented a product after not being able to find a solution to a particular problem. At Bubbler we actively supported other mums in business by running a Mums in Business newsletter each year, sharing stories of mums who have gone into business to support their family. They were always very well received.

If you don't have a large marketing budget, film your inspiration for starting your business and what you want to achieve with your community on your phone and then post it on your Facebook page. Your mums want to understand who you are, and what you believe in before transacting with you.

Tip 5 – Facilitate mum-to-mum recommendations

Your job as a marketer for your business is to facilitate a conversation where your Ideal Mum recommends your business to another Ideal Mum. It is a highly influential form of word-of-mouth advertising. You can post testimonials you have received from customers on a branded graphic background on your Facebook page. This demonstrates third party proof and acts as an endorsement for your business. If you are confident that you are delivering a quality experience or product for your clients, an easy way to achieve this is to turn on the ratings and reviews function in your Facebook settings. Then you need to encourage your existing customers to leave a review. You may wish to run a competition to highlight that you have turned on this function, inviting them to leave their review. A word of warning: you are unable to remove reviews or ratings that you deem unfavourable. In these situations, I recommend responding to the post at once and letting the customer know that you are happy for them to discuss their experience further and providing them with your contact details. Always leave negative posts on your page and respond courteously and promptly. It is a great opportunity to show how you deal with issues when they arise. It builds trust for prospective mums.

> 41% of Australians will inspect a brand's social media presence before making an online purchase if they have not purchased from their website before.
>
> *2016 Sensis Social Media Report*

Tip 6 – Use stories to sell

One key insight I've gained into Facebook is that mums like a softly softly approach when it comes to selling. At Bubbler, we worked with Sipahh flavouring straws on a four-month campaign. A well-known supermarket brand to many mums, Sipahh engaged us to assist them to drive awareness and sales to the new online store they were launching. We used an integrated approach across different mediums including newsletters and social media.

For the Facebook component we started with a direct sales post which went like this:

....

```
Have you seen the new Sipahh online store?

    These low sugar milk flavouring straws
come in 13 yummy flavours and will help
your kids enjoy more milk and less sugar
every day - Hello Marshmallow, Lamington
Dream and Chilled-Out Choc-Mint, just to
name a few. http://bit.ly/1MtCFSO

    To celebrate the launch of their online
store, Sipahh have a fantastic offer for
Bubbler members, buy 5 packs and get your
6th free. It's going to be hard to choose,
what flavour will you try first? Shop here
now:http://bit.ly/1MtCFSO

    Shop here now: http://bit.ly/1MtCFSO
```

....

Being open to trying some new strategies allowed us to divert from the direct sales message post and use a more native approach – where the brand was not the feature of the post. Instead it was incorporated into a true story which reflected the brand's attributes of having fun and discovering new things. The post went like this and featured an image of my three kids sipping from their Sipahh straws:

```
'You're not a bad dancer...... for a mum.'
(Master 10)
    Today Miss 7, Master 10, Miss 11 and I
had a Dance Off. My kids were teaching me
'the wave'. Apparently I need to work less
on my arms and focus on my shoulders.
    We celebrated our disco moves with the
new Hello Marshmallow-flavoured Sipahh milk
straw from our flavour crate we received
yesterday.
    It was a heavenly day with lots of fun.
    What was happening at your place today?
P.S. You can get a Sipahh flavour crate too
and save right here: http://bit.ly/1MtCFSO
```

The above post delivered four times more traffic to the Sipahh website than the direct sales post. By associating the Sipahh brand with me having fun with my kids, we significantly increased engagement and website traffic. Mums loved that they were able to identify with another mum who was struggling with her disco dancing with the kids. More so, they loved that I was showing them that it is okay to be silly with the kids and it really appealed to their sense of humour. Given the popularity and engagement this post generated, we went on and featured me having afternoon tea in a tree with my ten-year-old son, enjoying our favourite Sipahh flavours. My message is that your brand does not need to be the feature in a sales post for it to be evident and, in fact, the more you can include it in general storytelling, the greater your engagement and subsequent sales are likely to be.

ACTION

If you are already using Facebook go back and review how you are presenting your sales posts to your community. Is there a way that you could reframe your posts to include your brand attributes and show yourself? Start selling in stories.

Tip 7 – Build your list

Your objective should be to move your Facebook community over to your email list. You own your email list. It is a business asset and it is not subject to any changes Facebook might introduce in the future. Your email list is a great platform to sell from too.

You can encourage your Facebook community to sign up to your email list by installing the Sign Up call to action button on your Facebook cover page. You could also run a competition or offer a free gift that requires people to sign up to your email list as part of their entry and promote this on your Facebook page. Think about featuring a blog with useful, engaging content for your Ideal Mum and at the base of the blog have a newsletter sign-up button or alternatively use an app such as SumoMe which brings a pop-up or slider sign-up button onto your blog post. I consistently hear from other small businesses who blog regularly that this has been the single most important strategy they have implemented to build their list.

Tip 8 – Consistency

Consistency is key with your Ideal Mum. She is on Facebook frequently. I believe that you should be looking to do a minimum of one post each day, so seven posts a week. I post around 35 times each week during peak times. I may repost some content up to three times in a week, but the copy is slightly altered to ensure it's fresh to the reader who may be seeing it a second time. I recommend putting together a Facebook schedule each week to slot your posts. You should look to have a mix of engaging content, competitions and sales

Only 23% of small businesses are posting daily.

2016 Sensis Social Media Report

posts with the latter being no more than 30 per cent of your post content. You should be viewing your Page Insights to find out when your community is online and schedule posts accordingly. Automating your Facebook posts will save you loads of time. I use the Facebook scheduler and find it simple and easy to use. It's a great place to start. All the week's posts can be scheduled on the one day.

ACTION
If you already have a Facebook account for your business go into Page Insights and check if you have peak days and times. Set up your own promotional grid. It can be as simple as the one opposite.

Tip 9 – Facebook pixel

Facebook now offers a single pixel, in the form of JavaScript code, which allows you to build your community, measure your sales conversions, gain insights about your Ideal Mum's behaviour and measure performance of Facebook advertising. The Facebook pixel allows you to track someone who signs up to your newsletter, makes a purchase from your business or might register for an event you are running. It can help you identify which devices are being accessed prior to the transaction being made, providing you with greater insight about your customer's path to purchase. Best of all, the Facebook pixel allows

	Monday	Tuesday	Wednesday	Thursday	Friday	Saturday	Sunday
7am	Engagement	Engagement	Engagement	Engagement	Client Post	Engagement	Engagement
5pm	Blog – Recipe	Engagement	Blog – Recipe	Engagement	Engagement		
6pm	Engagement	Engagement	Engagement	Engagement	Engagement	Engagement	Engagement
7pm	Deal Feature	Deal Feature	Deal Feature	Deal Feature	Deal Feature	Engagement	Engagement
8pm	Deal Feature	Client Post	Client Feature	Deal Feature	Deal Feature	Deal Feature	Deal Feature

you to build an audience which you can then remarket with Facebook advertising to drive your sales conversions. There are full instructions on Facebook for Business for those businesses wanting to install the pixel.

LOOK AT THIS

KMART AUSTRALIA is one corporate brand that is doing an excellent job at targeting mums on Facebook. Their Facebook page has attracted more than 600,000 people. They use great visuals, have links to their own blog and answer customer enquiries promptly. Kmart engages mums with relevant content and encourages interaction with articles such as 'Kmart's best winter coats of all time'. They also have clear Facebook buttons making it easy to access their catalogue, sign up to their newsletter or complete a feedback form. One of the best things they have done is to feature items priced under $30, making them impulse buys and drawing mums into stores around the country. As a result, they have higher engagement on Facebook than some companies with more Facebook fans, according to a study by Online Circle Digital published in SmartCompany earlier this year.

GET SOCIAL: A high level of engagement with your Ideal Mum via social media is a great way to find out more about what she wants, while reinforcing your brand positioning.

CASE STUDY

AT BUBBLER, our experience has been that mums check Facebook first thing in the morning and then settle in for more prolonged use once the kids are in bed. We are able to periodically check when they are online by going into our page manager and clicking on Insights. This also identifies whether they are more likely to visit our Facebook page on any particular day. We actually find that the day of the week doesn't make much difference to mums when they access our Facebook page, but they show a clear preference for certain times of the day, with early morning and early evening onwards being peak periods. With this in mind, every Thursday we produce our social media schedule for the following week. This is a simple Word document with the days of the week running across the top and specific times down the left hand side. See page 157 for an example. We do five posts a day on weekdays and four posts a day on weekends. We post two sales posts each day and three engagement posts. These engagement posts are made up of things that we feel will be of interest to our community. They include recipes from our blog, funny memes, or interesting parenting articles we see trending online, as well as competitions.

GET SOCIAL: By getting to know the social media habits of your mums, you can tailor your communication to maximise their enagagement.

ACTION
Set up the Facebook pixel on your website. Visit the Facebook for Business page and search pixel for full instructions or, if you have the funds, outsource this job to a social media marketing specialist.

INSTAGRAM

Instagram is a growing social media platform for targeting mums, particularly those under 30 years of age. Given the way I see the tweens and teens engaging via Instagram, I believe that it will become an increasingly important social platform for all businesses targeting mums in years to come, along with SnapChat. In 2015, We Are Social, a social media agency, reported that there are 5 million active Instagram users each month in Australia. Unlike other countries, Australian women use Instagram more than men, according to a study undertaken by Datafication, a project which is analysing social media data in Australia to provide marketing insights, making Instagram activity something to consider. Facebook still dominates as Australian mums in general aren't as prolific with posts on Instagram – yet.

Instagram is a visual medium so it works best for businesses that focus on food, health and fitness, travel, fashion and music. Instagram provides mums with endless inspiration on what to eat, what to wear, how to decorate the house, provides nursery ideas and places to holiday. It is a treasure trove for many mums and many use it as a visual diary of their life. Despite this, small business has been slower to embrace Instagram with only 12 per cent of small businesses having an Instagram presence.

Instagram has none of the reach and algorithm changes which have driven many small business owners away from Facebook and, given its picture-based format, it is perfect for product-based businesses. If you have a service-based business, Instagram can work just as well, however you need to be more creative with your approach.

In order to ensure your Instagram success I am sharing my top seven Instagram tips.

Tip 1 – Great graphics

Instagram is a picture portfolio. It has the great ability to show off your products. Don't skimp on your graphics and look for interesting ways to present your products. Given we are targeting sales conversions, look to focus on predominantly presenting images of your smaller low-cost items which are easily shipped if you are an online business, to attract people to your website.

If you are not confident taking great images (which can be achieved on an iPhone, you don't need a fancy camera), then check out some of the images which you can access for little or no money. While most small business owners love Canva, I spoke to my designer friend

Kerrie Allen from Design Umbrella and she recommended picjumbo, Pexels, Death to the Stock Photo, Kaboompics and Picography, who all offer free images. If you have some funding, I have seen a client use a top photographer in their industry and produce hundreds of quality images in a half-day. Slowly rolling out the images has resulted in lots of new people joining their Instagram community.

Tip 2 – Use hashtags

A hashtag refers to words or phrases used on social media which start with the # symbol. The words or phrases used generally relate to the content in the post. Hashtags are used on both Facebook and Instagram but they are most commonly used on Instagram. There is much debate about how many hashtags to use, but as many people use Instagram like a search engine you need to choose relevant hashtags which will appeal to your Ideal Mum. You also need to include some of your keywords and your business name as a hashtag. I've spoken to lots of business owners and social media specialists and the jury is out on the ideal number. I've heard anything from three to 30 hashtags, but it seems the most successful are keeping their hashtags to a maximum of ten per post. Either way, use some hashtags to help mums discover you. I think the focus needs to be on including relevant hashtags including your brand name and tagline as a minimum, then consider hashtags relevant to the image you are posting and keywords you are using in the post. If you are starting out, consider checking out competitors in your industry and seeing what is performing well for them, or using popular hashtags. A word of caution though: choosing insanely popular ones can mean that your visibility becomes lost and you'll be missed. I think the key here is to choose relevant ones.

Don't think mums are all about buying slippers and dressing gowns. We can be intelligent people too and can see bullshit a mile away. Don't sugarcoat words. Being real and truthful will get more sales across the line.

#inmumswords

Tip 3 – Build your list

Just like with Facebook, you need to focus on getting your Instagram fans onto your email list also. You can use competitions to achieve this. I would strongly recommend partnering up with some complementary businesses targeting the same Ideal Mum and running a joint competition. This is a strategy I have successfully used to grow my database. It provides lots of interest and excitement and by running it with a number of complementary businesses, I am also being exposed to lots of new audiences.

Loop competitions are particularly popular, where a group of businesses get together and post an agreed competition graphic at exactly the same time. It requires the entrant to visit each Instagram page, like it and double tap on it, which takes you to the next business's page until you return to the start. I've seen lots of instances where loop competitions haven't worked because not all the businesses post at the right time, thereby breaking the loop, so if you ever consider participating in a loop competition know who you are working with and ensure they are as committed to the loop giveaway as you are. It goes without saying that you should be partnering with businesses who share the same Ideal Mum. When loop giveaways work, they can add hundreds of new followers to your account, however they are not without their risks.

Tip 4 – Interaction

You need to interact with people who come to your Instagram page. Leave thoughtful responses to their comments. It's a great way to build relationships and gain insights. I also believe you need to be active on other pages. Rather than just liking images on other pages, you can be seen by many more of your Ideal Mums by commenting on relevant Instagram profiles. I've seen many small business owners using the 20/20/20 or 30/30/30 rule where they like 20 photos, comment on 20 pages and follow 20 pages every day. It's a discipline, however they claim to reap rewards with higher sales from the activity.

Tip 5 – Show something different from your other platforms

Make Instagram different from your Facebook to encourage your community to interact with you on both platforms. Many successful businesses use Instagram to show their audience a behind-the-scenes look at their business. They make it more spontaneous but still keep it in line with their brand attributes. It still needs to have purpose. For example, you might want to photograph all the orders you have just packaged up to send out to customers or show all the boxes which might have arrived with your new season products to excite and motivate your Ideal Mum to come in store or head over to your website.

Tip 6 – Find your Instagram influencers

You need to seek out relevant social media influencers to work with you. These 'Insta Mums' might be bloggers, business people and those who have strong relationships and influence with their own community. You need to identify social influencers who target the same mum as you do. Comment on their posts, develop a rapport and look to partner with them in a joint marketing initiative.

Tip 7 – Maximise your Instagram profile

As Instagram does not allow you to have clickable links, you really need to maximise your Instagram profile which is located at the top of your account. I recommend that you have a concise description of what you do and include a unique bit.ly link to your website. This is a free service which allows you to shorten a web link. Most importantly, it allows you to measure how much traffic you send to your website from Instagram. Track results and if it's not working well, change your description until you find something which works.

CASE STUDY

FAT MUM SLIM is a community of mums aged 25–45 years. Chantelle Ellem is the creator and has built her Instagram following to almost 100,000. She believes that engaging with her audience and sharing relatable content with her community has been critical to her success. She is well known for creating the Photo A Day challenge which is highly interactive and designed to get people excited about photography. Chantelle recommends that if you are serious about growing your Instagram following, you should be looking to share two to four photos each and every day. She recommends spacing them out over the day and utilising Iconosquare or the Prime App to see what times your audience are online.

GET SOCIAL: Share relatable content on Instagram. Consider challenges to drive interaction and engagement with your community.

FLAT TUMMY TEA was launched in Perth in July 2013 by wife and husband, Bec and Tim Polmear. Flat Tummy Tea empowers women to get off their butts and take control of their health and prevent bloating by drinking all natural, herbal detox tea. I first met Bec when I was presenting at the League of Extraordinary Women in 2015 and I was super impressed with how she was using influencer marketing to successfully grow their Instagram community and, more importantly, drive sales of Flat Tummy Tea. In less than three years, Bec and Tim grew their Instagram community to 700,000 women globally before they sold and exited the business in April 2016. Bec believes that they were successful because they developed unique, engaging and valuable Instagram content for their target market. They also reached out to influential people online who had access to their target market and gave Flat Tummy Tea great exposure. Critical to their sales success was working out a way to quantify, measure and analyse the success of each Instagram post. This provided them with deeper insights and allowed them to deliver greater impact and improve sales conversions with subsequent Instagram posts. Bec believes it is not all about likes. 'Posting pictures of puppy dogs might get lots of likes but if it's irrelevant to your brand, what is it actually achieving? By doing so, you risk devaluing your brand and disengaging with your audience. Avoid clichés.'

GET SOCIAL: Track your results on Instagram and tailor your content to your Ideal Mum. Don't rely on people just liking a cute photo. Make social media work for you.

✔ CHECKLIST

- ⭕ Secure your Instagram name.
- ⭕ Write a short bio and ensure you have the bit.ly link set up to measure traffic.
- ⭕ Research relevant hashtags and start using them.
- ⭕ Post every day at times when your Ideal Mum will be accessing Instagram.
- ⭕ Review competitors in your industry and see what is working for them on Instagram.
- ⭕ Start sharpening your photography skills. Your iPhone is fine for taking great images, and use free graphics applications to overlay interesting quotes on images.
- ⭕ Start interacting with your community and other Instagram pages who have the same Ideal Mum. Interact every day.
- ⭕ Encourage people to use your hashtags by including them on your promotional materials and also do a post inviting people to use your hashtags.
- ⭕ Identify key influencers for your Ideal Mum. See if they work direct or approach their influencer agency and trial a campaign to assess the impact on sales.

ACTION
Go through and implement items on the checklist.

STEP 8: PROMOTE YOUR BUSINESS

Now you've done much of the hard work in building your assets, this final step is really all about accelerating your business connections to facilitate a sales conversion. I love the promotion stage because it is the time you can let your business shine.

I know that many small business owners are facing considerable budget limitations or are nervous about investing great sums of money because marketing hasn't worked in the past. If you have done the earlier work in steps 1 to 7 you can enjoy success with a limited investment or even for *free*. I'm going to show you the easiest way for you to appeal to your Ideal Mum and convince her that your product or service will solve her particular problems better than any other solutions in the marketplace.

I have identified eight promotional avenues that will increase your sales with an investment of no more than $300 each month. This list is not exhaustive by any means, but will deliver the most cost-effective marketing activities:

→ Testimonials, ratings and reviews
→ Publicity
→ Find your influencers
→ Podcasts, webinars and guest articles
→ Develop a compelling offer
→ Social media advertising
→ Leverage against bigger brands
→ Joint promotions

Testimonials, ratings and reviews

According to the Marketing to Mums survey, testimonials, ratings and reviews have the greatest influence on Australian mums when they're making a purchase for a product or service. Getting third party endorsement is a way for you to show social proof that your business is reputable, that your product works, that you do what you say you are going to do, that you exceed expectations and more. Testimonials allow you to build confidence, credibility and trust, demonstrate your competitive edge and overcome any scepticism your Ideal Mum might have about your product or service. The opinion is independent and therefore viewed upon as more trustworthy than the brand or business themselves.

63% of customers are more likely to make a purchase from a site which has user reviews.

iPerceptions, 2011

What are the characteristics of a good testimonial? A good testimonial doesn't just say that your business is awesome, it clearly addresses how your business successfully solved a problem and it reinforces your marketing claims. It will be successful if it focuses on the positive outcomes your Ideal Mum experienced as a result of working with you or purchasing your product. A good testimonial will also identify the writer of the testimonial. Rather than listing the writer as 'AM' it should say 'Amy Monroe, Melbourne', otherwise it is likely to come across as being fake or untrustworthy. A good testimonial will compare your product against another and identify yours as superior while stating why. A good testimonial is not from a supplier but a customer.

Your testimonial might be in writing, on audio or video. If you are running an event for mums, wouldn't it be great to capture their thoughts about your event and business as they left? These could be posted on your social media to promote future events. Mums love endorsements that are 'real' and not highly edited. It makes them appear more authentic and trustworthy.

There is an art to getting a good testimonial from your customers. Sometimes the conversational ones appear more effective than formal responses but how do you get those informal ones? Well, the Facebook ratings and reviews section is a start. Another way might be to ask your database why they signed up to your business. You'll gain some great insights and you might also receive some testimonials about how you have helped them.

> 68% of consumers trust reviews more when they see both good and bad scores, while 30% suspect censorship or faked reviews when they don't see any negative opinions on the page.
>
> *Graham Charlton, Econsultancy.com 2015*

Consider asking your customer base of mums to write reviews, testimonials and ratings on third party websites too. This proved to be very successful for Bubbler and brought with it considerable website traffic. Bubbler has been spoken about within forums on major parenting websites around the country and these third party endorsements provided my business with email sign-ups and subsequent sales without question.

Updating your testimonials on a regular basis is important also. Post them on Facebook and include them on your website, feature them in your media kit or marketing materials where appropriate.

Some small business owners I come across feel awkward asking for testimonials and rely on people providing unsolicited reviews and testimonials. If this describes you then I urge you to change this limiting belief and make a mind shift. Testimonials essentially allow your customers to sell for you. You need to be asking for testimonials often. Look at ways you can incorporate it into your everyday processes, perhaps a handwritten note in with your delivery packages reading 'Thank you for purchasing this product which I lovingly made. If you enjoy this product could you please take the time to share your experience on our Facebook page at ...' Another idea might be to ask for a testimonial when you are speaking with a client reviewing your service outcomes. 'Oh, that's great, Bill, it's good to hear that you received a 24 per cent increase in your sales as a result of our service. Could I ask you to write a few words about your experience and outcomes on our LinkedIn page?'

You need to be specific about what you are asking your customer to write about and step them through what you would like covered. Ideally you want someone to articulate the problem they were experiencing and how your business solved this problem for them.

You want to be selective about the testimonials you choose to promote on your website and marketing materials. Your aim is to demonstrate why your business is unique and to highlight other brand attributes you want to amplify. It is worthwhile ensuring that the testimonials you publish are from your Ideal Mum as this is more likely to speak to prospective customers.

Don't stress out about a bad testimonial. Research shows that it may actually make you appear more trustworthy. You just don't want too many bad reviews published. I would always advise not to delete poor feedback. A bad review or complaint is an opportunity for you to demonstrate how well your business can resolve issues and show your high level of care and attention to your Ideal Mum. Respond promptly, address the complaint specifically and show your solution. This will actually act to increase trust

Always ask your customer for permission to publish their testimonial.

and credibility in your brand as people see that you attend to issues when they arise. It is a particularly important cue when targeting mums. They expect and demand a high level of service. Most understand that issues arise in operating a business but they want to know that their complaint will be addressed promptly and satisfactorily. A poor review is your opportunity to demonstrate this.

CASE STUDY

THE BABY SLEEP COMPANY targets sleep-deprived mums with children aged under two years. Based in Queensland, Katie Forsythe and her team solve the problem of how to teach a baby to sleep. Her website has a dedicated page allocated to testimonials where she clearly identifies the name of the mum and the age of the baby. Each testimonial states how The Baby Sleep Company has solved a sleep problem and what positive difference this has made to the mum and baby's life. They have a number of children of different ages featured in the testimonials to appeal to mums in all different stages with their child.

RAVE REVIEWS: A great testimonial is one way of showing your business is trustworthy. For maximum effect, make sure the testimonials on your website indicate the problem your business solves.

CASE STUDY

PARADISE RESORT on the Gold Coast does an excellent job of allowing their customers to act as raving fans for their business, all at absolutely no cost. They collect testimonials to endorse their business via their Facebook page. This is the modern day 'word of mouth' and must surely be one of the most effective forms of advertising. Paradise Resort has received over 1700 reviews and has an average score of 4.4 out of 5. At the time of writing this book more than 1100 had given it a 5-star rating. The reviews are particularly compelling with one father declaring he had never written a review before but felt that he needed to share with other parents that this was 'the place to be if you have kids' and how 'there's so much for the kids to do … and so relaxing for parents'. The staff are described as being particularly helpful and friendly and he goes on to note that the only downside is that he is a smoker and needed to visit a special smoking room. What parent wouldn't be delighted to know that their children were not going to be subjected to passive smoking while holidaying? There are hundreds of these kinds of reviews throughout their Facebook review page with many of them talking about how they intend to go back or have holidayed there numerous times. This is advertising that Paradise Resort Gold Coast couldn't possibly buy, yet its influence on the decision-making of other mums, (as well as dads in this case) is extraordinary.

cont.

I see many businesses turn the Facebook review feature off, fearing that they will receive a bad review and be powerless to remove it from their page. I am a great believer that you allow the review and rating function to be on as it demonstrates a confidence in your business.

RAVE REVIEWS: Inviting responses from your customers via your Facebook page can give you the equivalent of advertising you can't buy. Customers who share their positive experience of your product or service can have a huge influence on potential customers.

I am less likely to buy a product if the advertisement features a pristine white house with children in it. These kinds of images intimidate me on a bad day, and make me think the advertiser has no brains on a good day.

#inmumswords

ACTION

Seek out testimonials from your best clients or customers. Email or call each client personally letting them know that you are updating your marketing materials and you'd like to invite them to send over a few sentences about their experience working with you. Be specific in your request, asking them to identify the problem they experienced prior to finding your business and how you were able to solve this for them. If you run an online store selling products, consider posting something on your Facebook page asking people to review your business and write to your top 20 purchasers personally via email asking them to share their experiences purchasing from your business.

Once you have these testimonials, include them on your website, in social media, on your brochures, in podcasts, webinars, anywhere where prospective Ideal Mums will see or hear them. Sharing testimonials on a regular basis should become part of your social media strategy.

Publicity

Many business owners are daunted and intimidated when it comes to seeking media coverage. Remember the media are looking for content and you need to think about your brand story and create reasons why the media would want to include you in their articles. Don't limit yourself to sending your media release to traditional media. There are plenty of channels you can tap into in the parenting industry, particularly online. Most importantly, you can do this yourself and the only cost is your time.

Before even considering approaching the media you need to develop your list of media contacts. You need to think about which media sources your Ideal Mum reads and watches. Go back to your avatar and identify the publications you want to target. Consider featuring on webinars, podcasts and guest blogging. You may want to look to offer your product or service as a prize for businesses who share your Ideal Mum.

I found that features appearing online rather than in print resulted in greater sign-ups to my database and more subsequent sales. It was easy for my Ideal Mum to click once to take them from the article to my website, rather than reading about me and then having to type my website into her phone. This is one of the key reasons I stopped engaging in print advertising at Bubbler. I would recommend all online businesses look to target online media where your details are only one click away.

Twitter is great for interacting with the media, potential investors, and other entrepreneurs. This is where you should be doing your online networking. It's where you can develop your relationships with the journalists you have now identified and become their go-to person for your particular industry.

Another avenue is to register for free media leads service SourceBottle. This service sends you twice-daily emails filled with media opportunities and is used by journalists and bloggers to find subject-matter experts to quote or provide comment in a story. It's free to register and I've seen many businesses get great coverage responding to a call-out from a journalist or blogger. I have featured on Channel 7 News and *Today Tonight* as a direct response to SourceBottle call-outs.

Bec Derrington, the founder of SourceBottle, has a number of hacks to help you get results:

1. Respond within the first hour (if possible) of receiving SourceBottle's 'Drink Up!' email alert. Your alert will contain call-outs on the topics you've indicated you're interested in. Cast your eye over it for relevant media leads as soon as it hits your inbox. Why? Because even if the deadline is a few days away, the journalist will pull the call-out as soon as a suitable source gets in touch.

2. Don't answer the call-out in full in your response. It's more important for you to show why you're the best person to interview than it is to answer every question.

3. Ensure that your contact details are accurate. If not, the effort you've made to respond to the journalist or blogger is likely to be in vain. Why? Because if your email address bounces or the telephone number

you've provided isn't correct, they may not take the time to work out what it should be. Not only that, it can create doubt about your credibility as a source, since they can't verify the details you've provided.

4. 'Show your hand.' If you're responding to a call out for 'dietitians with 5+ years' experience to discuss the impact of dairy foods on the diet', say, it's best to clarify that you satisfy the journalist's prerequisites, and to then highlight your opinion with respect to dairy foods in the diet. For example, 'I am a dietitian with ten years' experience based in Melbourne. I have strong views on the inflammatory nature of dairy foods and their impact on the diet, particularly for women approaching menopause ... I have written a number of articles on dairy products in the common Western diet here [insert hyperlink]. I'm happy to talk with you any time this week. My number is ...' Stating your opinion makes you desired talent. Simple.

I have found the following tips to work well in approaching the media to secure a story:

→ Create an eye-catching title for your media release to get their attention. This might be an interesting statistic or a play on words to give them a reason to read your information.

→ Tell the journalist how what you do helps their readers or viewers. Remember that it's not all about you.

→ Piggyback onto an existing story.

→ Incorporate statistics from recent reports.

→ Give them the whole story – consider other sources the journalist could use too. This is where it is sometimes helpful to partner with another business owner.

LOOK AT THIS

Ruslan **KOGAN** is a master at making a splash and doing things in an unconventional manner which results in his business getting great cut-through. Kogan is Australia's premier online shopping destination and when the first bricks-and-mortar pop-up store was launched in Melbourne, he made a very humorous video about applying online shopping methods instore. The video went viral which was the aim of the exercise, I'm sure. I shared it myself amongst my community. It allowed a huge number of people to view his video and know that he had now launched a Kogan pop-up store. He created his own publicity at significantly less expense than if he went to a PR firm.

In my first year of business with **BUBBLER** I had a chance encounter with a freelance media specialist at a conference. A bit later, I engaged her services and she taught me about connecting with the media. As a former Fairfax marketing employee, she was able to share with me what angles would best fit to secure a story in a mainstream newspaper. I learned first that I needed to be very strategic. I had to write my media release according to the media I wanted to feature in, rather than having a one-size-fits-all approach. I needed to understand where my story would fit in their structure, and subsequently which journalist to target. This resulted in my business being the lead story for WAtoday.com.au and then becoming the lead small business story for Fairfax online, appearing in Sydney, Melbourne, Brisbane and Canberra. From there it caught the eye of *Today Tonight* and they went on to feature a story about me and my business the following week.

GET PUBLICITY: Do your homework and be smart about how you target media coverage for your business.

ACTION

→ Make a list of all the media your Ideal Mum uses. Identify the most popular and the journalists who write about your industry segment.

→ Set up a Twitter account and follow the identified media outlets and journalists covering your industry. Comment, like and consider sharing their relevant articles to develop a relationship with them.

→ Sign up to SourceBottle to receive twice daily newsletters with journalist call-outs.

→ Write your media release. It should be less than one page including contact information, with the most important information in the first paragraph or two of the media release as not everyone is going to read the entire document. Use simple language free from jargon and provide the journalist with quotes they can use in the article. Please ensure you have quality high-resolution images of yourself for use and state this at the bottom of the release along with your contact details.

→ Make sure you are available to answer calls after you send out your media release. Journalists will quickly overlook you if you are not available when they call.

Find your influencers

A mum's world is changing. We already know that she relies more on mum-to-mum recommendations and she is digesting her information differently to previous generations thanks to her increasingly busy life and the arrival of the smartphone and internet. She is engaging online with key people who have influence over her decision-making.

Over the past five years I have watched the growth of online mum communities. Many bloggers and business pages catering for Australian mums have considerable influence over their community and there is huge opportunity if you can tap into the power of their influence on their audience to grow your business.

66% of mums belong to social media groups which are just for mums.

Marketing to Mums survey 2016

You need to find influencers who have the same Ideal Mum as you. The influencer might be closer than you think. Many times you have raving fans who are existing customers who have great influence over other mums. When I started Bubbler in Perth, I found an influencer in Caprice Burrows, a mum of four who runs a blog called Perth Kidz which helps mums find fun things to do with their kids. She was very supportive of the Bubbler business and spoke to her community about the upcoming launch of our business which resulted in spikes in our email subscribers and Facebook community.

You might find suitable influencers on Instagram, Facebook and in the general community who will advocate and provide that third party endorsement. I strongly recommend that you look at entering into a long-term relationship which is why identifying them from within your own ranks is always preferable. You might provide a monetary payment, bonus products or something else to reward your influencer. It might be as simple as thanking them and giving them more of your time. *The Age* reported that BellaBox, an Australian beauty subscription box with a healthy seven-figure turnover, 'spends anything between $50 and $5000 for an influencer to write a post about its products'. As a small business owner there are likely to be growing, engaged communities where you can pay more reasonable amounts. The key focus is not on the size of the community but the level of engagement. You can judge an influencer's engagement by clicking on their Facebook page number of total likes and it will reveal how many people are talking about them. You can also view the level of interaction on their social media pages and blog, if they have one.

Big businesses are really embracing influencer marketing. The head of marketing from Qantas recently confirmed that they will direct more than half of their media budget into social and digital channels at the expense of traditional media. These activities include using influencers. Other large businesses who are using influencer marketing to promote their brands include Country Road, L'Oreal and Mercedes Benz.

I would consider engaging with an influencer in a joint competition. This will expose your business to a whole new database of mums who form your target audience. You might wish to provide your product as the prize or, if you are a service provider, look to negotiate a third party to be involved and donate the prize. You just need to make sure that the prize is highly desired by your Ideal Mum.

Another idea is to have an influencer be the guest poster on your page for a day or a week. They can then promote this to their community. This has two mutually beneficial outcomes: the influencer is being exposed to your community and you are being exposed to their community.

Use less pink and more of the other lively non-pastel colours. I don't like pink and am bombarded with it everywhere I go.

#inmumswords

Jo Whitton of **QUIRKY COOKING** is a top Australian food blogger sharing tips and recipes for delicious healing food and happy, healthy living. Jo is a mum herself, and has built a community of more than 300,000 people across social media and her database, mostly mums who are looking for a healthier way to live. She has been flown around the country and overseas to conduct cooking demonstrations and has also published an allergy-friendly cookbook for Thermomix. Jo was recently invited to team up with some fellow influential food and wellness bloggers calling themselves the Aussie Wellness Women. Together they have created a joint cookbook, *From Our Kitchen to Yours*, with all proceeds being donated to the Luke Batty Foundation. To date they have raised $40,000. The foundation helps women and children who are affected by family violence, a cause important to many mothers. Jo holds considerable influence over her audience and in this case she could use that influence to contribute to a very worthwhile cause. It is not surprising that she is frequently approached to post about products and services operating within the wellness space. Through Marketing to Mums, I engaged her services for one of my clients which resulted in a significant sales lift.

GOOD INFLUENCERS: Think about who might help to spread your word, because mums respond to influencer marketing.

> **ACTION**
> Research who the influencers are in your Ideal Mum's world. Start following and interacting with them on social media. Send them your product or invite them to experience your service. Have no expectation with this; you are wanting to develop a relationship with your identified influencers. Once a relationship is established and you feel they are the right fit for your brand, look to engage them through a post, campaign or competition to their community. These should be timed so you are only running one competition at a time; if you don't dilute your focus you can measure the impact of each influencer's activity.

Podcasts, webinars and guest articles

If you are a service-based business, I would focus heavily on promoting your business by first promoting you. By increasing your profile, you are seen to be the go-to person within the industry. Share your knowledge in guest podcasts, webinars, speaking engagements and by writing guest articles for the media your Ideal Mum follows.

Look to leave your audience with a way to follow up with you. This is not necessarily the place to make an offer but you tell viewers or listeners that there is lots more free content on the subject available on your website or specific landing page where you could also promote an introductory offer.

CASE STUDY

In launching my new consulting business, **MARKETING TO MUMS**, I have featured on both Australian and overseas podcasts, acted as a consultant to an international mastermind group of ten small businesses and started writing a fortnightly article for Smallville.com.au, a hub for small business owners who think big. I have been booked to deliver a workshop at the AusMumpreneur Conference where I will be selling copies of my book to my ideal client. These activities raise my profile as a consultant who specialises in helping businesses of all sizes sell more to mums.

BROADCAST YOUR BUSINESS: Let people know who you are and what you can offer via a range of media – use free content to direct potential clients to your service or product.

ACTION

Identify potential podcasts, webinars and media that your Ideal Mum regularly digests. Make a list and write to them to share how you could assist their community. In addition to this spend some time seriously considering launching your own podcast, webinar series or events where you can raise your profile amongst your Ideal Mum audience.

Develop a compelling offer

One of the areas I see businesses struggle with is recognising what their Ideal Mum values and knowing what to offer. One of the first things we do when we work with a new client is to understand their marketing objectives. Once these are clear we can assist them to put together an offer which our community of mums will find compelling and will maximise conversions for our client. We have found that conversions are not related to how big the discount is, rather it is around our Ideal Mum's perception of value. We have had great success with brands who reduced their products by only 15 or 20 per cent rather than 50 per cent. You could offer free shipping for a day or celebrate winning an award and take 10 per cent off all products for one day only. Focus on what makes you unique in all your advertising campaigns and ensure a strong call to action. Your offer should always only be available for a limited time. I generally don't recommend more than five days as you want your mum to take immediate action rather than having it fall into her 'I'll do that later on' pile which rarely gets actioned.

> **ACTION**
> Brainstorm some sales promotion ideas you could run for both your existing clientele and sales promotions targeting your Ideal Mum on other sites.

CASE STUDY

LITTLE BENTO WORLD has Australia's largest range of lunchboxes, bento boxes and bento accessories and it's a go-to place for mums in the know. At Bubbler, we ran a 20%-off storewide exclusive sales promotion for them soon after we launched our advertising platform. They were wanting to raise awareness and lift sales amongst a wider group of Australian mums. This discounted sales offer was limited to five days and our customers needed to use a special promo code at the website checkout page. It resulted in one category of lunchboxes selling out on the first night. Most customers purchased two or more items delivering an above average shopping order of $65 per customer. We sent 1327 clicks through to their website from the social media posts alone and Little Bento World reported a significant lift in sales and attracted new clients to their business. We have subsequently run successful short-term sales offers for as little as 15% off and delivered great results.

MAKE AN OFFER: Know what your Ideal Mum wants, and tailor offers to fit what she values most.

Social media advertising

With many algorithm changes on Facebook over the past two years, businesses are reporting a significant drop in organic traffic. Facebook is now very much a 'pay to play' platform. It seems an inevitability that many brands must advertise to maintain their reach. I have seen that, with practice, social media advertising can provide a good return on investment but there can be lots of trial and error to go through first.

To increase the likelihood of success, I recommend you ensure you use high resolution, good quality images which show people using your products rather than the product by itself. You need to select your visual with mobile in mind as this is where most mums will see it. I would give consideration to trialling advertising using video as this has been shown to increase engagement, click-throughs and ultimately sales conversions.

When engaging in Facebook advertising it is important you target your Ideal Mum using the ad targeting options, and the copy of your advertisement should have a headline which is going to grab her attention and feature appealing content. Make sure when they click on your advertisement that you are sending them to a landing page which has a relevant offer or call to action. This may be a free gift in exchange for their email, remembering you first need to develop a relationship rather than going for the immediate sale.

Leverage against bigger brands

One way you can position yourself and raise your profile at the same time is by leveraging bigger brands. Ruslan Kogan is an excellent example of someone who significantly raised his profile and that of his business by engaging in a public conversation with Harvey Norman over price and importing goods from overseas. Gerry Harvey got all hot under the collar each time he was asked to comment on Kogan's low-cost TVs and it propelled Kogan into our living rooms with plenty of free coverage on *A Current Affair* and *Today Tonight*. He strategically leveraged against a much bigger business to get publicity and connect with a much larger audience.

> **ACTION**
> Identify five larger brands or businesses which have a similar Ideal Mum. Think creatively about how you could leverage against each of these brands or businesses to raise your profile or the awareness of your business.

Joint promotions

Joint promotions are an excellent way to promote your business and drive sales. By working with complementary businesses who share your Ideal Mum but are not in competition with your business, you can significantly increase your exposure to your target market at insignificant prices.

I have frequently run joint competitions with the aim of building my database. These typically will see my business being exposed to 150,000 or more of my ideal customer for the cost of $50 for the graphics. How do I do this? I negotiate with a select number of complementary businesses I would like to work with. I also identify a prize which I believe will be greatly desired by my Ideal Mum. This does not necessarily mean a highly priced item – the emphasis is on *desired*. As part of the mode of entry, require entrants to sign up to your free newsletter. This then allows you to commence a relationship with these mums. Please note that you need to understand the legal requirements of running a competition and I strongly suggest contacting the state legislative bodies to get advice.

part 3

HOW TO IMPLEMENT THE 8 PILLARS OF SUCCESS

Critical to the success of any business is that they deliver a robust customer value proposition (CVP) through a marketing mix of price, product, position and promotion. Over the past 12 months, I have come to realise how powerful my 8 Pillars of Success can be in delivering CVP and driving sales and growth within a business. In October 2015 I started consulting with a client and by implementing my program, I have delivered them a 655 per cent increase in revenue compared to the same time the previous year.

I'm sharing our success with you as a case study to highlight how I approach the implementation of my eight-pillar program when consulting with a client. I will take you through our process and the key outcomes so you can better understand how you might do the same for your business.

CASE STUDY: PRANA CHAI

Prana Chai is an artisan chai company in Melbourne, founded by three charismatic and experienced cafe operators, Vincent, Mario and Koray. They had created an outstanding chai product which they hand made fresh every morning with eight all-natural ingredients. The Prana Chai recipe is based on a loose leaf tea mixed with spices and natural bushland Australian honey, and provides a welcome relief from some of the powder- and syrup-based chai in the market.

Prana Chai has established an extensive wholesale business with a seven-figure turnover and, at the time I commenced consulting to them, their chai was being served in several thousand cafes across Australia and abroad. They were enjoying a period of great growth, having expanded into the US and European markets. Prana Chai had been selling direct since 2014 and they were organically growing the online retail section of their business at 52 per cent. Lacking time and expertise in the mum market, they engaged Marketing to Mums with a view to accelerating direct sales here in Australia. My consulting brief was to drive their online direct sales channel via a new segment niche targeting mums. This would allow the directors time to focus on expansion into Asia and support their growing North American and European operations.

In consulting to Prana Chai, my approach was to embed myself within the business one day each week over an eight month period. This onsite consulting approach allowed for direct channels of communication with the owners and facilitated agile implementation of agreed strategic marketing initiatives. I like to work this way as it makes me feel part of their team and it can also provide valuable insights about the business. I can pick up valuable information that they might feel is incidental and really educate my client about mums and make changes to the way they look at this powerful market segment.

Process method

I use a five-step process methodology ensuring that my program, insights, and expertise are interwoven in a strategic marketing direction specific to the goals and objectives of my client.

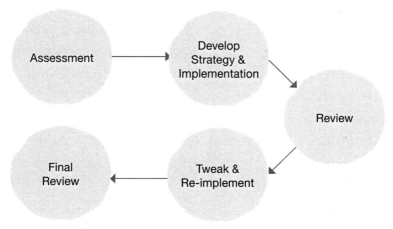

Ideally this process would be carried out over a 12-month period where I work with the business for a day each week.

Assessment

The first thing I did was immerse myself in the business and assess the current situation. For those familiar with design thinking, this was essentially the empathy stage where I needed to understand what my client really wanted to achieve through this project. I also needed to understand exactly how Prana Chai was performing against each of the eight pillars in order to identify opportunities for growth and what obstacles were in the way. Effectively, I was looking to perform a gap analysis – where they were and where they wanted to be at the end of the project, allowing me to understand what I needed to do to get them there.

Assessment 1 – Ideal Mum

I conducted five methods of research to determine Prana Chai's Ideal Mum. Knowing the importance of correctly identifying their target market, I wanted to invest considerable time and effort in this stage. Over four weeks I did the following:

1. Interviewed the founders
2. Surveyed existing direct customers
3. Interviewed top 20 baristas and cafe owners
4. Surveyed mums via Bubbler database
5. Spoke with health-conscious mums

It was apparent the founders of Prana Chai thought their target market was aspirational, health-conscious women in their late twenties. I then undertook a survey of their existing database. The Prana Chai community are very engaged and we received more than 60 per cent open rate on our survey request. This is unheard of and speaks volumes about their customer base's loyalty and willingness to help. As the sample size was still relatively small it was important to do further investigation. I next interviewed the baristas and/or owners of the top 20 cafe stockists of Prana Chai. I held open conversations to ascertain who they felt was ordering Prana Chai in their cafe. I also concurrently ran an independent survey through the Bubbler community of 150,000 mums to gain more understanding about their chai drinking habits, motivations and preferences, and spoke with mums one-on-one in my networks to ensure we were sampling a broad range of different mums.

> It is the little personalised touches to a product or service that would make me choose one over another.
>
> #inmumswords

What I uncovered was that Prana Chai's Ideal Mum for their online sales channel differed from those who drank Prana Chai in cafes. The mum who purchases Prana Chai online is more likely to be older than those who drink it in cafes. This was a critical finding because if we had chased the 'cafe mum' I do not believe we would have enjoyed the same success, as our marketing efforts would have been poorly directed.

Prana Chai's Ideal Mum for the direct sales channel was more correctly identified as being aged 35–54 years. She drinks chai primarily for the taste and has a strong preference for the tea leaf chai offerings, and she also loves the sensory experience chai delivers. This customer perceives chai to be a healthier alternative to coffee and believes it makes her feel good and relaxed. Facebook is her preferred social media platform but she also spends some time on Instagram and Pinterest. She is time poor and not aspirational. She is aware that she needs to care for herself in order to provide for the rest of her family. Her cup of Prana Chai gives her five minutes of 'me time' and she can brew chai at a time convenient to her.

Assessment 2 – Brand story

Prana Chai had done an excellent job at creating their brand story. They shared the story of how Vincent and Mario, childhood school friends, had travelled the world for many years. They shared their first experience of drinking chai in the Subcontinent, before they opened a cafe together in St Kilda called Inka 7. They spoke of how they met Koray, a regular in their cafe, and how they experimented making their own chai to remind them of their travels. They shared how it became so popular in their cafe, how they went on to purchase another cafe with space big enough so they could make chai to supply to a growing number of cafes around Melbourne, and soon interstate, before they outgrew the enormous cafe and set up Prana Chai headquarters making and supplying their chai. This story had already been widely communicated via notable cafe industry publications such as Broadsheet, The Urban List and Bon Appétit.

They talked about their chai being an honest, natural product which is hand-made with love. They clearly displayed their story on their website, however it was not shared on any other mediums. They had made a video explaining how they make the product which showed their personalities and allowed people to get to know them but again, this was available on their website only.

Assessment 3 – Market positioning

Prana Chai wants to be seen as the leading loose leaf chai tea provider in the world. They want to be known for their honest, natural, premium product which is not compromised in any way. They have an excellent reputation amongst the cafe industry which is growing their wholesale business, however through the surveys with mums I discovered there was low awareness of their brand. Those who tried the product were easily converted but not enough of their newly identified Ideal Mums even knew the product existed – they were not likely to be reading lifestyle and cafe industry publications, and they weren't aware of the brand story.

It was high on my list to change this situation.

Assessment 4 – Customer experience

Once the Ideal Mum was identified I was able to assess how the existing Prana Chai product range, customer service policy and brand communications were being received. I looked at the business through their Ideal Mum's eyes. I did an audit of the buying process on the website by making a purchase myself. I checked it from both a desktop and a mobile for performance. Key things I noted:

→ absence of testimonials

→ stronger call to action required

→ duplicated information on the purchase page which caused some confusion.

I immediately noted that it was unlikely that their Ideal Mum would have all the right equipment to brew a great cup of Prana Chai at home. Without a pot and strainer, she was not likely to recreate the chai at its best so this reduced the likelihood of repeat purchase. I also noted that it was difficult to access the video instructions on how to brew the product at home. It was imperative that marketing efforts be directed towards ensuring mums had the right equipment and knew how to correctly brew the product so that it tasted at its best and they would purchase again.

During my discussions with the founders they expressed frustrations that many of their direct orders were one-off purchases or customers were taking months to re-order so I set one of my objectives to shorten the sales cycle so people were purchasing Prana Chai online more regularly.

Assessment 5 – Find partners

While the founders are well known and connected with many other boutique artisan brands in Australia, they lacked time to place a focus on building partnerships. There were some ad hoc marketing partnerships but I identified there was a great opportunity to create and execute mutually beneficial marketing partnerships.

Assessment 6 – Build the list

The building of their list was limited to people who had purchased Prana Chai online before. There was no newsletter in place and therefore no sign-up option on their website or on social media. In short, there were no clear efforts to grow their database or to form relationships with their Ideal Mum and drive sales.

Assessment 7 – Get social

Prana Chai had two very clear customer segments: their wholesale clients and their direct customers who were end users. In reviewing Prana Chai's social media, I identified a need to accommodate two customer segments and increase their social media activity. Prana Chai had a social media presence on Facebook and Instagram but it appeared mainly directed at their cafe stockists. There were few communication tools being used to develop relationships with the Ideal Mum customer. There was a need to identify how we would develop each segment through social media without ostracising the other segment.

The identification of the Ideal Mum for Prana Chai had major implications for their marketing strategy.

I like reading reviews, testimonials and experiences from other real mums so incorporating these into advertising would likely sway my opinion and might encourage me to try the product.

#inmumswords

Immediately I knew that Facebook would be the primary social media platform for this mum. It was significantly more important than Instagram. We decided at this point to run Instagram as the primary platform for the cafe customers and Facebook to develop relationships with their Ideal Mums.

Assessment 8 – Promote

Promotional monies had been invested in creating two great videos, one on the story of Prana Chai, the other on how to make Prana Chai at home. However, there was very little promotion of Prana Chai to their Ideal Mum as this had not been a focus in the past because of limited resources. Efforts to date had been small occasional sponsorship activities on request. As a result, awareness of their brand was low amongst their Ideal Mums.

Develop strategy and implementation

With a clear understanding of how Prana Chai was performing against each of the pillars, I developed a strategy document to address these gaps and make real connections with their Ideal Mum to drive sales conversions and shorten the buying cycle.

The strategy document was summarised by a marketing activity timetable which provided an easy reference page to see the strategy mapped out.

The five key activities I identified were:

1. Increasing awareness of Prana Chai amongst Ideal Mums

2. Addressing obstacles to purchase

3. Showing other uses for the product to reduce length of sales cycle

4. Developing relationships with social influencers to fuel growth

5. Developing relationships with the Ideal Mum via social and third party endorsement

Increasing awareness of Prana Chai

One of my first tasks was to look at increasing the awareness of Prana Chai amongst the Ideal Mum community. I primarily did this through product sampling amongst parenting communities which had a high proportion of Prana Chai's Ideal Mum. We knew that there was a high conversion of mums who tried the product to purchase the product. Wanting to minimise marketing investment I looked at the subscription box industry where you can typically provide the samples and they cover the distribution of product via their monthly or seasonal gift boxes. It avoided costly postage rates and allowed supporting promotional materials about Prana Chai to be communicated also.

Addressing obstacles to purchase

I was concerned that Prana Chai's Ideal Mum would not have the pot and strainer at home to brew their Prana Chai and I knew this would be a barrier to purchase. Vincent had already pointed out that brewing in a saucepan would not result in the same cafe taste so it was critical to ensure that the mums had the right equipment. We already knew that it was also difficult to access the video instructions on how to brew Prana Chai at home.

So we launched the Prana Chai Gift Box. This box contained Prana Chai Masala Blend, a Prana Pot, stainless steel strainer and a mug. It was our objective to ensure that this was the first purchase the Prana Chai Ideal Mum would make when shopping online, which would ensure she had the best equipment to brew her chai at home. We did this through a competitive price point. The gift box contained almost $70 of value but we launched it at $39. We brought the Prana Chai Gift Box to market quickly in early December to test its performance as a Christmas gift. We also supported the launch of the Prana Chai Gift Box through a small number of competitions with suitable social communities and advertising on Prana Chai's own website.

Showing other uses for the product

I wanted to shorten the sales cycle of buying Prana Chai online and address the founders' concerns about people purchasing as a one-off buy. I recommended we develop an A5 recipe booklet which would share the Prana Chai story, show people how to brew Prana Chai at home and share six recipes for cooking with Prana Chai. This booklet was a longer-term project as it first required recipes to be developed, professional photographs to be taken and a professional designer and printer to be identified. We didn't get this to market until May when we launched it as a bonus in the Prana Chai Gift Box. It was very well received by Prana Chai's Ideal Mum. We published a link to the recipe booklet on the Prana Chai website so existing customers can access and experience cooking with Prana Chai. We shared recipes with other businesses for publication along with our samples to encourage mums to cook with the product.

We have also formed relationships with food bloggers who are also mums and have strong communities of Prana Chai's Ideal Mum, to develop recipes that we both share amongst our respective communities. This has benefits for both businesses.

Developing relationships with social influencers

I identified the most important communities who were aligned with Prana Chai's values and Prana Chai's Ideal Mum and we commenced building relationships with them. Initially that involved sending them some product to try. This was without any expectation, however many often shared with their communities. This progressed to running competitions and in some cases, they created recipes using Prana Chai which they published to their tribes. Each time a social influencer endorsed or made reference to Prana Chai we saw spikes in orders.

Developing relationships with the Ideal Mum via social and third party endorsement

We ran a review campaign with a large parenting website, Mum Central, where we gave away 15 Prana Chai Gift Boxes to people we identified as Prana Chai's Ideal Mum. The campaign started with a review by Mum Central themselves, a feature on the Prana Chai Gift Box and a call-out for mums to review the product. We received over 450 applications and selected 15 reviewers across the country. These reviews by real mums were then published in an article via the Mum Central community of more than 500,000 mums. The activity served to raise awareness of Prana Chai and provide a large volume of product testimonials. We were then able to share these testimonials as third party endorsements on Prana Chai's Facebook page each week. It has effectively provided content that can be repurposed and communicated in other mediums to reach our Ideal Mum.

I recognised the value of building Facebook as the primary social media platform for Prana Chai. We set about using Facebook to develop relationships with our Ideal Mum to grow the retail business and Instagram

Advertisers need to get a few good reviews from mums and have these mums post about the product on Facebook. Then watch the word spread like wildfire as other mums purchase the same product.
#inmumswords

to develop relationships with Prana Chai's wholesale accounts, cafes. We turned on ratings and reviews on Facebook to encourage mums to leave their reviews about Prana Chai and rate them. To support this we ran a small competition encouraging people to share their experience with Prana Chai. We also shared third party content others posted about Prana Chai. This included cafes but also tips and recipes from other mums.

Review

Over four months we issued over 3000 samples across four different providers. Each activity was supported with social media and/or promotional support specifically of Prana Chai. Awareness levels can be trickier to measure and the founders felt that the sampling was not yielding a direct sales response. They wanted to invest these monies in other marketing efforts which yielded an immediate sales result. We agreed to stop sampling and looked to raise awareness of Prana Chai through social influencers and earmarked this marketing investment to be allocated to joint collaborations with other artisan brands.

Within four months of implementing the new strategy, Prana Chai had featured in many of our desired social influencers communities. Website traffic had lifted significantly. Sales were up, led by the success of the Prana Chai Gift Box. Not resting on our laurels, we wanted to see what we could do to improve the gift box offering. We had experienced unreliable supply on the mug soon after launch and I felt that the mug didn't really reflect the premium offering so we started to look elsewhere.

Tweak

We improved the Prana Chai Gift Box by doing two things. Firstly, we replaced the mug with a Robert Gordon chai latte mug. Robert Gordon is a Melbourne based family business with great quality products so it was a good fit for Prana Chai. While these cost more, we recognised that they were highly desired by our Ideal Mum, it was instantly recognisable and it removed the supply issues experienced over the Christmas period. The other improvement we made was the addition of the recipe booklet. This ensured that people knew how to brew Prana Chai at home and also offered them ideas on how they could cook with it. It was a premium-looking booklet with professional photography and graphics which we added at no extra charge so the perceived value of the box increased also.

We heightened activities in April in the lead-up to Mother's Day, which we believed would be a peak selling period. We also undertook a trial selling Prana Chai Gift Boxes through cafes and identified that we will look at the speciality foods retail market in coming months.

We improved the social media interaction with quality lifestyle and product images being taken by one of Australia's top food photographers. We featured mums with small children in many of the lifestyle images and we also shot a series of how to brew Prana Chai at home making it more relatable to Prana Chai's Ideal Mum.

The other tweak we made was to the website. Koray rebuilt the website with a better focus on story flow and an improved path to purchase. This also had internal benefits for Prana Chai as it provided an easier backend to manage the other international businesses as well. Some further tweaks were identified to improve the customer experience on their website, to be rolled out in coming months.

Final review

So what results did we achieve? By implementing the 8 Pillars of Success into the Prana Chai marketing strategy, direct online sales were up 655 per cent on the same period last year. I was able to accelerate this growth from an average 52 per cent prior to consulting commencing to an average 509 per cent within eight months of starting the Prana Chai project. Awareness has grown significantly amongst their Ideal Mum segment and I established the direct sales channel as a business in itself. I have demonstrated to my client the value of mums as a powerful market segment and shown them a new way to communicate and grow relationships to better understand mums' needs and desires.

So successful has the contract been that I have been invited to roll out the program in the US, Europe, South-East Asia, Canada and Japan over the next 12 months to develop Prana Chai's online sales efforts in targeting mums. The Prana Chai Gift Box will be standardised globally and launched in the US and Japan in August 2016. The Prana Chai newsletter will be launched allowing Prana Chai to strengthen the relationship and foster brand loyalty with their Ideal Mum and allowing the founders to share their story and journey towards achieving their vision.

I have shared this in-depth case study with you so you can understand how the 8 Pillars of Success might be implemented into an existing business. No matter what size your business is, there are benefits to investing the time to roll out this program.

20 QUICK WINS

I passionately believe that mums wield enormous power in our economy. There is a new way to communicate with mums that recognises their influence on the buying process for almost everything. Be warned though, mums are increasingly becoming more aware. Social media really has brought about an enormous shift and great empowerment for mums as consumers, and they are becoming more vocal as time goes on. While as a mother this delights me, it presents an enormous challenge to businesses. I am confident, however, that by utilising the 8 Pillars of Success framework you will gain a greater understanding of your customer or client. Armed with this greater knowledge and insight, you will be able to serve your Ideal Mum better, and in turn she will deliver you increased sales and growth.

My eight-step framework takes a longer-term view of how to increase your sales to mums. I recognise, however, that many small businesses need to get new customers in fast. For those of you looking for quick wins, I have compiled 20 ways to deliver you more sales to mums. After a few quick wins, I guarantee you will want to start putting the 8 Pillars of Success into effect in your business.

This checklist also serves as a reminder of what you've learnt throughout the book – refer to it every few weeks to see what you could be doing better, or more often. These are all things you'll be doing in your business if you follow my 8 Pillars of Success, but if you pick a couple of them to implement sooner rather than later, you can get some impressive results fast.

✔ CHECKLIST

1. Demonstrate social proof – promote your third party endorsements including awards, testimonials, ratings and reviews.

2. Share your brand story – show your passion for why you do what you do.

3. Identify and engage your mum influencers – run a competition, ask them to review your product or service. Reward them. Develop an ambassador program.

4. Develop a compelling offer – it needs to be something that your mum will perceive as good value, it should be in limited quantities or run for a limited time as mums hate to miss out.

5. Tap into your networks and organise to exchange advertising services. You might exchange Facebook posts, Instagram or banner ads on your respective websites.

6. Communicate to your existing customers regularly and promote your offer through all your channels including website, newsletter, instore and social media. Existing customers are more likely to open your emails, read your social media posts, take your calls and subsequently purchase your product than communicate with a new business. They already know you.

7. Focus on promoting the solution rather than your product or service. You will increase your conversions if you share how your Ideal Mum might feel or benefit from using your product or service.

8. Thank your mum after each purchase. Consider a handwritten card, a follow-up phone call or some other method to show you care about her and her contribution to your business.

9. Reward mums who frequently purchase from you. Send out an email to tell them how much you appreciate them and that you'd like to offer them a 10 per cent discount coupon/code on their next purchase. Ensure it has an expiry of 30 days to encourage immediate action. Alternatively, give them a bonus or sample product to try.

10. Have a charity night where 5–10 per cent of sales are donated to a cause which is important to your mum.

11. Consider an offer that provides a follow-up sale. For example: 'Purchase $75 worth of goods and receive $25 voucher.'

12. Bundle your products and offer a discounted package.

13. Make the purchase process easier. Your Ideal Mum is busy, don't put obstacles in her way. For example, offer PayPal so she doesn't have to get off the couch in the evening to get her credit card when she is ordering on her phone, or minimise the page clicks she needs to do online or allow her to order online and collect instore.

14. Promote your unique selling proposition. She will love you for your differences.

15. Introduce or promote your free trial or money-back guarantee to reduce the perceived risk in purchasing from or working with you.

16. Promote your referral program to your existing customers. This enables them to recommend you to their friends and facilitates a mum-to-mum recommendation.

17. Run a joint competition with another business to build your list. You can then start developing a relationship with that business and subsequently sell to their database.

18. Package your goods and services with a complementary business and ensure both businesses promote it.

19. Enter awards – it's not only a great opportunity to be recognised, but it can build trust and deliver media attention.

20. Seek publicity – run a monthly media release schedule.

The 20 Quick Wins checklist is available for download at www.marketingtomums.com.au so you can print it out and use it as a daily reminder of what you should be doing in your business to attract mums.

I would love to hear your feedback about what worked in your business. Please post your wins on our Facebook page at **www.facebook.com/marketingtomums** or send me an email to **katrina@marketingtomums.com.au**

About the author

Katrina McCarter is the founder and CEO of Marketing to Mums, a research and marketing consultancy. She is a marketing strategist who specialises in helping businesses sell more to Australia's most powerful consumer, mums.

With a Bachelor of Business (Marketing) and a Masters of Business Administration (International Business), Katrina lives and breathes sales and marketing strategy. Her career covers the corporate sector as well as small business, and she is the mother of three children aged 13, 11 and nine, all of which means she knows firsthand how important mums are to commerce. She is highly regarded for her creative growth strategies and her ability to negotiate strategic partnerships, and works with both small and big businesses to increase sales and profits selling to mums.

In January 2012, Katrina launched Bubbler.com.au an online shopping website promoting the best shopping offers for mums, working with remarkable brands such as Bonds, Adairs, Booktopia and ABC Reading Eggs. Over a four-year period, she grew Bubbler to a community of more than 150,000 mums without ever spending more than $300 a month on marketing. Bubbler won national awards for excellence in social media and customer service. In September 2016 Katrina will release a comprehensive survey report looking at Australian mums' social media habits and how they want to be marketed to. These deep insights garnered from more than 1800 mums provide ground-breaking learnings for businesses wanting to target mums.

Katrina is a regular contributor to business media including Smallville.com.au and has been featured on *Today Tonight* and in *The Age* and *Sydney Morning Herald*, *The Brisbane Times* and SmartCompany. She is a thought leader who is regularly called upon as an inspiring speaker at world-class events, and is the marketing mentor for the Women's Business School, launched in June 2016.

To work with Katrina, have her speak at your event or to enquire about the survey report, please contact her at Marketing to Mums on 0427 161 677 or email: katrina@marketingtomums.com.au

Acknowledgements

Bringing a book to life requires a team. I have been extremely fortunate to have an excellent group of people supporting me at home, in business and in life.

To my husband, Dave, thanks for all the encouragement in times when things got challenging. I appreciate you believing in me and for your support of my entrepreneurial endeavours.

To my children, Lucy, Josh and Alice, thanks for pitching in and cooking dinner, folding the laundry and putting yourself to bed on nights when I was working on this book. Long may it continue ☺. Whatever you do, dream big and follow whatever makes your heart sing – I hope you are inspired to write your own book one day.

Where would I be without the grandparents? Mum, Dad, Wendy and René, thank you for coming to the rescue and supporting our family to allow me more time for writing after work. I am deeply grateful.

Andrew Griffiths, when you told me it was time to write a book and share my insights and experience, I was excited and nervous. It has been an enlightening process to unpack my skills and experience, formulate my framework and share it with the world. You have always provided motivation, inspiration and constructive feedback, ensuring that I am very proud of this book. Thank you.

To my investors, thank you for giving me the business opportunity and backing me. I have garnered incredible insights into the workings of small businesses and what converts mums into customers. It really has been instrumental in launching Marketing to Mums. Thanks for taking a chance on me.

I started researching this book almost 18 months ago and I would like to thank all the small business owners I interviewed, and those who agreed to feature as case studies or who shared their tips. This helped me better understand what problems you were experiencing in marketing to mothers.

To the 1800 or so mums around the country who participated in the Marketing to Mums survey, I am eternally grateful. Your level of dissatisfaction and your call for change in the way businesses market their products and services came across loud and clear. I am deeply committed to assisting businesses to make these changes, and in doing so, accelerate their growth.

To my clients, both past and present, thank you for trusting me with the strategic direction of your businesses. I would like to make special mention of Mario, Koray and Vincent from Prana Chai who agreed to share their story of working with me and implementing my methodology. Nothing is more powerful than sharing stories to inspire others to make changes in their own business.

To my publishing team, Andrea McNamara and

Dijana Dawe, thank you for the wonderful opportunity to work with you both. Your knowledge, experience and insights were warmly welcomed by this first-time author. I could not have asked for more suitable and professional publishing experts to guide me through the process. Thanks also to other authors who generously answered all my questions along the way.

Special mention goes to Julia Kuris from Designerbility who created the book cover. Julia was always willing to make changes and tweak it until it was perfect. Another designer, Kerrie Allen from Design Umbrella, has been instrumental in my businesses over the past five years. Thank you for your support.

I am extremely grateful to RMIT University academics Dr Kevin Argus and Dr Christine Murphy, who critically reviewed my manuscript, along with the numerous colleagues and entrepreneurs who wrote testimonials about me or this book. I feel very humbled and honoured.

To my fellow entrepreneurs, you keep me energised, focused and ready to soar. I love being surrounded by passionate, positive people. Thanks also to my accountability team who kept me focused throughout this process.

And to you, the reader, thank you for reading this book. I hope I have delivered key insights for you that will allow you to strengthen your relationship with mums and, in turn, grow your business.

References

Part One

Page 6: 'Mums control $132 billion in consumer spending'; 'Marketing to Australian Mums', Canadean, 2011

Page 6: Mums are largest contributor to GDP; 'The Smart-Mum Phenomenon', CampaignBrief, Reborn & Lion Co., online article, 18 February 2014; http://www.campaignbrief.com/2014/02/reborn-lion-co-uncover-how-bra.html

Page 6: '6,227,200 mums in Australia with a further 140,000 women becoming mothers every year'; Australian Bureau of Statistics, July 2016

Page 7: 'Women are entering the small business world at twice the rate of men'; 'More Australian women starting their own business than ever', Scarr, Lanai, *Herald Sun*, 4 September 2015; www.heraldsun.com.au/news/national/more-australian-women-starting-their-own-businesses-than-ever/news-story/3ab4cfac6d2f2951e4cf656bef80ee8f

Page 34: '80 per cent of women aged 25–54 years have a smartphone'; 'Connecting with the modern Australian Mum', Read, Min, Marketingmag, online article, 21 February 2014; www.marketingmag.com.au/news-c/infographic-connecting-with-the-modern-australian-mum/

Page 34: '37 per cent of desktop buyers browsing the retailer's site use other devices prior to purchase'; 'It's a Cross-Device World: Criteo's Q4 Mobile Commerce Report Reveals Top Companies Bet Big on Mobile Consumers', Criteo press release, 17 February 2016; www.criteo.com/news/press-releases/2016/02/q4-mobile-commerce-report-reveals-top-companies-bet-big-on-mobile-consumers/

Page 37: Complaint to Target about tramp-like clothing for young girls; 'Social-media mums, "Batman" of the internet', Tuohy, Wendy, *Herald Sun*, blog post, 14 August 2012; blogs.news.com.au/heraldsun/theperch/index.php/heraldsun/comments/i_am_social_media_mum_hear_me_roar/

Page 37: 'online consumers are not just buyers anymore'; 'The Eight Touchpoints of a Customer's Consideration Phase', Gonzalez, A, MarketingProfs blog, 25 February 2014; www.marketingprofs.com/opinions/2014/24455/the-eight-touchpoints-of-a-customers-consideration-phase

Page 39: Fuck You, Mother's Day blog article; 'Fuck You, Mother's Day', Fuck You Friday blog, 7 May 2016; fuckyoufriday.com.au/fuck-you-mothers-day/

Page 45: 'online retailing accounts for more than $16 billion'; 'Online Shopping in Australia: Market Research Report', IBISWorld, online report, March 2016; www.ibisworld.com.au/industry/default.aspx?indid=1837

Page 45: 'mobile searches have overtaken desktop queries'; 'It's official: Mobile devices surpass PCs in online retail', Siwicki, B, Internet Retailer blog, 1 October 2013; www.internetretailer.com/2013/10/01/its-official-mobile-devices-surpass-pcs-online-retail

Page 50: Pregnant mums are twice as likely to be seeking information online; 'Did you know pregnant women access blogs twice as much as non-pregnant women?', Kids Business, online article, 26 March 2015; kidsbusiness.com.au/did-you-know-pregnant-women-access-blogs-twice-as-much-as-non-pregnant-women/

Page 50: Medela's survey of Australian mums who seek parenting advice online: 'Mums Leading the Information Generation', Kid Magazine blog, 6 May 2016; kidmagazine.com.au/mums-leading-information-generation/

Page 53: 'criteria for making a purchase decision change dramatically once a woman becomes a mum'; 'Motherhood Changes Shopping Habits', Marketing Charts, online article, 10 November 2011; www.marketingcharts.com/uncategorized/motherhood-changes-shopping-habits-20017/

Page 53: 'An engaging story has been scientifically proven to connect with mum'; 'Why Storytelling is Scientifically Proven to Boost Sales', Carlozo, Lou, Yesware blog; www.yesware.com/blog/storytelling-drives-sales/

Page 55: '91 per cent of women felt misrepresented and misunderstood by advertisers'; 'What Women Want From Marketers: Straight Talk', Curtis, Janie, Forbes Magazine, online article, 22 April 2009; www.forbes.com/2009/04/22/selling-women-curtis-cmo-network-curtis.html

Page 56: 48 per cent of women in Australia and New Zealand are size 14 or above; 'The Shape Report 2011: Revealing what men and women think about women's bodies', Australia and New Zealand Market Research, Triumph, online report, March 2011; www.abc.net.au/mediawatch/transcripts/1106_shape.pdf

Page 57: '74 per cent of respondents claiming they weren't aspiring to mothering perfection'; 'The Truth About Mums', Saatchi & Saatchi, online report, 2014; http://saatchi.co.uk/uploads/140984300765298/original.pdf

Page 58: Increase in marketing messages since the 1970s; 'How many ads do we see a day? Do you remember any?', Yankelovich Consumer Research, Walker-Smith, Jay, online article, 19 March 2014; unomarcomms.com/our-insights/glenn/how-many-ads-do-we-see-day-do-you-remember/

Page 61: '48 per cent of small and 54 per cent of medium businesses have a social media presence'; 'How Australian people and businesses are using social media', Sensis Social Media Report 2016, page 55, 1 June 2016; www.sensis.com.au/assets/PDFdirectory/Sensis_Social_Media_Report_2016.PDF

Part Two

Page 69: How gender impacts thinking; 'Tale of Two Brains', Gungor, Mark, online video, 2008; https://www.youtube.com/watch?v=Rww_p8CO37U

Page 71: '90 per cent of the purchase decision has already been made in the unconscious'; '90 Percent Of All Purchasing Decisions Are Made Subconsciously', Lindstrom, Martin, Ispo blog, January 2015; mag.ispo.com/2015/01/90-percent-of-all-purchasing-decisions-are-made-subconsciously/?lang=en

Page 79: 'People don't buy what you sell'; 'Start with Why: How Great Leaders Inspire Action', Sinek, Simon, online video, 2009; www.youtube.com/watch?v=u4ZoJKF_VuA

Page 90: Jeffrey Lant's seven-touch rule; 'How Many Contacts Does it Take Before Someone Buys Your Product?', Business Insider Australia, Cityroom, 13 July 2011; www.businessinsider.com.au/how-many-contacts-does-it-take-before-someone-buys-your-product-2011-7

Page 104: '83% of retailers say customer experience is very important to business strategy'; 'CommBank Retail Insights', edition 2, online report, 2016, page 10; www.commbank.com.au/content/dam/commbank/ business/pds/retail-insights-report-edition-2.pdf

Page 112: '21 per cent sales increase with the addition of a money-back guarantee'; '5 brand strategies to uniquely position your ecommerce business above the competition', Schreiber, Tucker, Shopify blog, 15 January 2015; www.shopify.com.au/blog/16692816-5-brand-strategies-to-uniquely-position-your-ecommerce-business-above-the-competition

Page 113: Segmentation increases click-throughs; 'Commerce Marketing Gurus: Top 2016 Trends', Bronto online report; mkto.bronto.com/ rs/797-YXJ-932/images/WP_2016_Trends_Strategies_v1.pdf

Page 114: Retail businesses should do more to personalise the shopping experience; CommBank Retail Insights', edition 2, online report, 2016, page 17; www.commbank.com.au/content/dam/commbank/ business/ pds/retail-insights-report-edition-2.pdf

Page 114: Link between customer experience and female employees in leadership roles; 'CommBank Retail Insights', edition 2, online report, 2016, page 20; www.commbank.com.au/content/dam/commbank/ business/pds/retail-insights-report-edition-2.pdf

Page 130: Four-step process of growing your email list; '4 Steps to an Effective Facebook Sales Funnel', Loomer, Jon, Jon Loomer blog, 4 September 2013; http://www.jonloomer.com/2013/09/04/facebook-sales-funnel/

Page 135: Building email list by increasing email capture methods; 'How we doubled email sign ups in 30 days: Our strategies to get more email subscribers', Lee, Kevan, Buffer blog, 14 August 2014; blog.bufferapp. com/get-more-email-subscribers-how-we-doubled-email-signups

Page 139: 'Australians are spending 24 minutes each time they check in to Facebook'; 'How Australian people and businesses are using social media', Sensis Social Media Report 2016, page 4, 1 June 2016; www.sensis.com.

au/assets/PDFdirectory/Sensis_Social_Media_Report_2016.PDF

Page 139: '78 per cent of Australian mums were checking Facebook every day'; Facebook Australia Users Demographics, March 2012; http://searcheverywhere.net/facebook-australia-usage-statistics-march-2012/

Page 139: '40 per cent of Australian women are accessing their social media while watching TV'; 'How Australian people and businesses are using social media', Sensis Social Media Report 2016, page 33, 1 June 2016; www.sensis.com.au/assets/PDFdirectory/Sensis_Social_Media_Report_2016.PDF

Page 140: Benefits of as little as 6 hours per week invested in social media marketing; '2015 Social Media Marketing Industry Report: How Marketers Are Using Social Media to Grow Their Businesses', Stelzner, Michael A, Social Media Examiner, May 2015, pages 19 and 21; www.socialmediaexaminer.com/SocialMediaMarketingIndustryReport2015.pdf

Page 141: Large businesses have grasped the social media opportunity; 'How Australian people and businesses are using social media', Sensis Social Media Report 2016, page 55, 1 June 2016; www.sensis.com.au/assets/PDFdirectory/Sensis_Social_Media_Report_2016.PDF

Page 141: '31 per cent of small businesses ...; 'How Australian people and businesses are using social media', Sensis Social Media Report 2016, page 69, 1 June 2016; www.sensis.com.au/assets/PDFdirectory/Sensis_Social_Media_Report_2016.PDF

Page 143: '9 million of these are accessing Facebook via a mobile'; 'These incredible stats show exactly how huge Facebook is in Australia', Heber, Alex, Business Insider Australia, 8 April 2015; www.businessinsider.com.au/these-incredible-stats-show-exactly-how-huge-facebook-is-in-australia-2015-4

Page 146: Real Morning Report on Facebook; 'Organic Balance: Real Morning Report', online video, 11 April 2016; www.youtube.com/watch?v=bh19YxASA-4

Page 151: '41% of Australians will inspect a brand's social media presence ...'; Sensis Social Media Report 2016, page 43, 1 June 2016

Page 158: Kmart case study; 'The most popular brands on Facebook in Australia revealed'; study by Online Circle Digital, Keating, Eloise, 3 February 2016; http://www.smartcompany.com.au/marketing/62677-the-most-popular-brands-on-facebook-in-australia-revealed/

Page 160: '5 million active Instagram users each month in Australia; We Are Social's Tuesday Tune-Up #189, Lane, Harriet, 12 May 2015; wearesocial.com/au/blog/2015/05/socials-tuesday-tune-189

Page 160: Australian women use Instagram more than men; 'The Secret Life of Social Video', Nicol, D, online report, datafication.com.au/socialvideo/

Page 161: '12 per cent of small businesses having an Instagram presence'; 'The Secret Life of Social Video', Nicol, D, online report; datafication.com.au/socialvideo/

Page 170: '63% of customers are more likely to make a purchase from a site which has user reviews'; 'Ecommerce consumer reviews: why you need them and how to use them', Charlton, Graham, Econsultancy blog, 8 July 2015; https://econsultancy.com/blog/9366-ecommerce-consumer-reviews-why-you-need-them-and-how-to-use-them/

Page 171: '68% of consumers trust reviews more when they see both good and bad scores ...'; Econsultancy blog, 8 July 2015, as above

Page 185: BellaBox; 'Meet the new breed of super influencers', Jones, Kate, *The Sydney Morning Herald*, 22 February 2016; www.smh.com.au/small-business/smallbiz-marketing/social-media-influencers-the-new-marketing-darlings-20160217-gmx2y2.html

Page 185: Large businesses using influencer marketing; 'Influencers cash in on social media's power', Morgan, Elysse, 24 March 2016; www.abc.net.au/news/2016-03-24/influencers-cash-in-on-social-media-power/7274678